THOSE LEGENDARY MEN OF THE WILD WEST

A PICTORIAL HISTORY
by
Phyllis Zauner

ZANEL PUBLICATIONS
P. O. Box 1387
Sonoma, CA 95476

Other ZANEL Publications:

California Gold, Story of the Rush to Riches
Carson City, Capital of Nevada
Lake Tahoe, The Way It Was Then and Now
Sacramento and the California Delta
San Francisco, The Way It Was Then and Now
The Cowboy, An American Legend
Those Spirited Women of the Early West
Virginia City, Its History...Its Ghosts

Copyright 1998
All rights reserved
ISBN 0-936914-24-6

FRONT COVER
Poster for Buffalo Bill's Wild
West show; Black Bart holds up
the stage; "Wild Bill" Hickok
calls the cheat.

BACK COVER
Judge Roy Bean holds court

CONTENTS

The Wild West was a unique American experience, which still fascinates the world, creating a spirit that remains with us.

The men who wove the rich fabric of the history of the States and Territories during those times, whether outlaws, lawmen or simply heroic survivors, became the legends which gave us the incomparable American West.

– The Author

Why was the West so Wild?

The Wild West, scene of gunfighters' exploits, roistering cowboys, and rampaging killers, is as much a part of America's folklore as are its innumerable characters whose adventures have thrilled a world-wide audience for more than a century.

The mold for the "Western man" was cast by the Texas Rangers, a ragatag lot with long, matted hair and scraggly beards who looked like cutthroats but whose exploits were heroic.

It might further be said that the "Western man" was conceived when Samuel Colt patented his first revolver; that he was tested in the wild-and-wooly California Gold Rush where stagecoaches bearing the mines' output rode through country as wild as the times.

But he came into his own after the Civil War that spawned the majority of the outlaw gangs that festered in these trail-end towns. Boys like Frank and Jesse James, the Younger brothers and "Bloody Bill" Anderson were graduates of Quantrill's Raiders, a band of skilled Confederate guerillas whose leader taught his men the hit-and-run techniques they later used so successfully as criminals.

The atrocities committed by William Quantrill and his men were so bloody and brutal they earned the state the name of "Bleeding Kansas." Frank James was one of 450 raiders who descended on Lawrence, Kansas one dawn and shot every man and boy in sight, then put the town to the torch—an assault unparalleled for its savagery.

Yet in spite of the fact these outlaws killed many innocent people, they were seen by many Southerners in a kindly light as modern-day Robin Hoods. They were, in effect, acting out the revenge fantasies of hundreds of thousands of people who had lost a war, lost friends and relatives, lost a way of life.

A second factor contributing to the lawlessness of the Wild West was the sheer vastness of it.

When the nearest friendly person might be a hundred miles away, almost every man wore a six-shooter on his hip to protect his life and property. There was no other law. If a man's cattle were stolen, his crops destroyed, or he and his family attacked, it was up to him to track down the culprits.

The vastness of the open land also worked in favor of the fugitive. A man on the run had many things in his favor. Provided he got a head start from the scene of his crime, the chance of capture and punishment was remote. He could change his name and disappear into the wilderness of Texas, the deserts of Nevada, or the mountains of Colorado.

Communication was extremely limited in those early days, too. Months might pass before information about a wanted man reached his pursuers. By then, of course, he could be well beyond reach.

With so little working against him, a man disposed to a life of crime would see little need to walk behind a ragged-eared mule and a plow when there was easier money to be taken from the hated banks and railroads.

There have been other great wide-open spaces, other vast, thinly populated areas, but nowhere else in the world has there been the peculiar vitality, the savage turbulence, and the rip-roaring drama of the long-drawn-out struggle for law and order in the American West.

The question that remains is: "Why is it so glamorous, so full of romantic legend?"

The answer probably lies in the fact that the West was not "romantic" to the Westerner who lived the times, but to the Easterner who could not ride a horse across the plains, could not wear a six-shooter, or swagger down a wooden sidewalk in high-heeled boots. It was the Eastern journalist, novelist and sketch artist (and later, Hollywood moviemaker) who have given the harsh frontier life an aura of colorful, adventuresome fantasy.

The image of the "good" bad man as a sort of Robin Hood was largely established by novelists who treated outlaws with considerable sympathy and, aware that no one is all good or all bad, found sufficient reason to excuse his faults.

A more realistic approach suggests the need to distinguish between the man who killed out of meanness and the man who became an outlaw because he believed there was no other way for him to ensure that no one would take unfair advantage of him.

Most men who carried a gun were neither heroic supermen nor dastardly villains. Rather, they were human beings in violent times, exceptional only in their readiness to kill if necessary to save their own hide, and having the right technique to do so.

The real bad man, the outlaw killer, was willing to steal and kill to get what he wanted. He had no scruples to speak of and believed that his needs and wants came first. Although he may not have been entirely responsible for his behavior, having been born in an era of violence, yet he rarely tried to improve his relationship with society.

He was not a difficult man to spot. Treading the thin line between life and death made him a more than cautious individual. He avoided dark alleyways and the direct glare of street lamps. Indoors he kept a wall behind his back. The most renowned gunmen were all compulsive travelers, hard men to keep track of.

In general, the gunfighter's life lacked the patina of glamor that has been laid upon it. Said a Texas Ranger, "I know most of them, and the life those fellows are leading in the mesquite shrub to keep out of reach of the law is a dog's life. They ought to thank me for giving them a chance to come in and take their medicine."

Gunmen of the Wild West lived by a code of sorts, which went as follows:

- Shoot an unarmed man and it counts as murder.
- If he is armed, even if facing the wrong way or sound asleep, you will probably get away with a plea of self-defense at your trial.
- The dead man's friends, however, may lynch or shoot you.

"See?" He's armed."

Those who aspired to a gunfighter's career could look forward to spending endless hours learning the trade. In later life, Bat Masterson described the work that went in to perfecting the skills that enabled a man to "throw lead" quick and straight, as though by instinct: "To accustom his hands to the pistols of those days, the man who coveted a reputation started in early and practiced with them just as a card shark practices with his cards, as a shell game man drills his fingers to manipulate the elusive pea, or a juggler must practice to acquire proficiency. When he could draw, cock and fire all in one smooth lightning-quick movement, he could then detach his mind from that movement and concentrate on accuracy."

The hand dexterity required to achieve such proficiency was enough to discourage all but the most dedicated aspirants. The gun had to be grasped by its handle with the wrist twisted downward, while the finger reached down at a 45-degree angle for the trigger, and the thumb cocked the hammer.

Reputations of the most renowned gunfighters were often considerably inflated. Bat Masterson was supposed to have dispatched a dozen men while he was a sheriff. There is no real evidence he shot anyone. Wyatt Earp's record rests largely on the episode at the OK Corral. The most bald-faced liar among the gunmen probably was Wild Bill Hickok. But within the gunfighter breed, there was little interest in setting the record straight, for notoriety gave them an edge in a duel with a nervous opponent. They often honed this edge by embellishing their past deeds.

The gunfighter of fact and fiction is now firmly established in American folklore, whether his role as a desperado was romanticized or his actual deeds chilling. The dust from the last cattle drive has long since settled; the trails and sun-baked streets the gunfighter traveled are no more. But his ghost still rides, and the legends he left behind are cut deep into the American heritage.

John Wesley Hardin, the fabled gunfighter, became incensed by the snoring of a man in the room next to his in the American House Hotel in Abilene, TX. Not one to waste time with his feelings, Hardin began firing his gun through the bedroom wall. The first bullet awoke the stranger, the second one killed him. Years later, Hardin tried to set the record straight. "They tell lots of lies about me," he complained. "They say I killed six or seven men for snoring. Well, it ain't true, I only killed one." Regardless of the number, Hardin certainly diminished the population of snorers in Texas.

Jesse James
The James-Younger Gang

It was a cold February afternoon in Liberty, Missouri, and few people were on the streets to witness the arrival of a dozen rough-looking men on horseback.

Three of the men dismounted at the town square, the rest pulled up in front of the bank. Two got down and entered the bank.

Handing the teller a $10 bill, one of the strangers said, "Change this bill." Then, as a sort of afterthought, he added, "I'd like all the money in the bank."

The startled teller, momentarily stunned, hesitated. The stranger gave him a shove with his gun in the direction of the vault, and watched while a grain sack was filled with gold and silver coins.

Meanwhile, the second robber was waving his gun around, asking where the paper money might be. "There, in the box," quavered a clerk. Paper got stuffed in with coins, the two bank men were shoved into the vault, and the gang of robbers galloped out of town, whooping and hollering, shooting a pedestrian who got in their way. The day's take was over sixty thousand dollars.

It was the first armed daytime bank robbery ever. And the innovative perpetrators were Jesse and Frank James.

A strange legend has built up around Jesse James. Even as he and his brother and their outlaw friends murdered innocent people, they were becoming heroes. According to folklore, Jesse never failed to distribute his stolen loot among weeping widows; old men freezing in the snow received with grateful thanks his proffered coat. He was the eternally handsome youth riding across western plains, the bag of gold—stolen, of course, from the hated banks and railroads—tied to the pommel of his saddle, while far behind, hidden by his dust, came the hopelessly outclassed pursuers.

Theodore Roosevelt, under the mistaken impression that Jesse James was robbing from the rich to give to the poor, called the outlaw the Robin Hood of America.

There is no evidence that any money was ever given to save a widow's home; Jesse firmly believed charity begins at home.

He was a strange man with a dark streak of violence running through his makeup. Like his brother and the Younger brothers who later joined him, he had been trained by Charles Quantrill, leader of Missouri's largest guerrilla band following the Civil War—a man who had truly earned his title as the "bloodiest man in American history." All the tactics of guerrilla warfare would be incorporated in Jesse's later *modus operandi* as an outlaw.

He knew each man of his group intimately. The scene of every robbery was carefully reconnoitered. He knew the layout of the town, the number and caliber of peace officers, the getaway routes, the total assets of the bank or train. His men were superb riders, and experts, from their guerrilla tactics, at "busting a town."

At the start it wasn't all easy going. They sometimes had disappointing hauls, learning that bankers could be almost as stingy with robbers as with farmers.

In one town, when they galloped into the town square, yelling wildly and firing pistols in the air, a teller locked the vault. Townsfolk fired on them, and kept up a hunt for escaped outlaws for months. Jesse and Frank got away, but three of their comrades were caught and lynched.

Moving their business to Kentucky in hope of easier takings, they met with another disappointment, with one of their gang hauled off to jail. So they decided to go home to Mom in Clay County, Missouri.

Mom was quite a woman, steadfast and pious, now remarried to a doctor. In her entire lifetime, she never failed to stand up for her boys. There at home, Frank, an avid reader, spent his days reading Shakespeare. Jesse got baptized and prayed long and hard for the forgiveness of his sins.

But it wasn't long before the boys were back to business, asking a bank cashier to change a $100 bill. Then, an unlucky coincidence occurred. Jesse thought the cashier looked like a Union officer who had killed his buddy in the war. Wrenching the bill form the man, he shot him and scooped up $700 from the open safe. A gunfight with local citizens ensued, Jesse's foot got caught in his saddle as he rode off. Frank rescued him, but they had been recognized and their name came up in the paper.

Three years after the James Gang robbery of the Liberty Bank, Mrs. Zerelda Samuel, mother of Jesse and Frank, came into the bank and attempted to pay off a loan with revenue stamps taken in the robbery. It was reported that she became "indignant" when she was forced to pay in cash.

Jesse wrote to the newspaper, "I have lived as a peaceable citizen, obeying the laws of the United States, ever since the war." With that dignified declaration of innocence, he launched what was to become, in effect, a lengthy public relations campaign. Thereafter, he often wrote to newspapers disclaiming any responsibility for all the crimes attributed to him.

Over the next decade, the James brothers and the four Younger brothers — Cole, Jim, John and Bob — robbed dozens of banks and trains, always managing somehow to outwit the law and the Pinkerton detectives who were constantly on their trail.

Once they slipped over to Iowa to rob the bank at Corydon. They got little more than $5,000, a sizable sum for those days, but far short of the $40,000 that legend has credited to them. They had, however, made a memorable impression on Corydon, for when they had grabbed the loot, they rode to a church where most of the populace was gathered for a political rally. Jesse interrupted the proceedings by

hollering to the thunderstruck citizens, "We've just been down to the bank and taken every dollar in the till." With a couple of whoops and a wave of their hats, they galloped off.

They played to an even larger crowd at the Kansas City annual fair. Seizing the cashbox, they made off with the largest day's receipts, some $10,000, then spurred their horses through the crowd, unfortunately trampling to death a 10-year-old girl.

The _Kansas City Times_ ran the story front-page, of course. And the next day they carried the usual letter from Jesse, denying that he and his brother had been anywhere near the fair.

Strangely, the general public believed him.

They wanted to. The James boys were seen as Southern farm boys, still standing for the lost Confederate cause, gallant and defiant. And in those postwar years, farmers, desperate for funds to restore their ravaged lands, developed a strong hatred for the banks who denied loans or charged outrageous interest rates.

This stage holdup in Kentucky actually took place exactly as shown. One passenger's watch was later recovered in Jesse's home.

When the Pinkerton Detective Agency was called in by the banks to settle the hash of the outlaws, the local constituency was more likely to go with the James letters-to-the-editor. Thus Pinkerton agents ran up against a stone wall. Not only did they get little help, they didn't really know what the James brothers looked like.

They recognized the signs though. On one train holdup, Jesse James brought up a little laughter when, with typical wry humor, he asked the passengers, "Where is Mr. Pinkerton?"

On another train robbery, just before leaving the train with everyone's personal effects, Jesse handed a note to the conductor. "Here, give this to the newspaper," he said. It was, in effect, a news release describing the "most daring robbery on record," with deliberately misleading descriptions of the robbers. The Pinkerton agency was left with little doubt who had engineered the heist.

$25,000 REWARD
JESSE JAMES
DEAD OR ALIVE

$15,000 REWARD FOR FRANK JAMES

$5000 Reward for any Known Member of the James Band

The James gang of hoodlums, taken at Kansas City during one of their periodical sprees, shows Cole and Bob Younger standing, Frank and James seated. Their abundant armament was typical of their calling.

The James-Younger gang couldn't seem to lose. Everything they did worked fine. Everything the Pinkerton men did turned out wrong.

One agent, posing as a local, was quickly spotted by the gang, and killed. Agents stormed the home of Frank's father-in-law — a futile attempt since the man hated Frank and would never have let him in the house.

Finally, in desperation, the Pinkerton agency installed an agent as a "farm hand" in a house across the road from the James farm. When the agent spotted the James boys there, he sent for a force of detectives to storm the place. Surrounding the house, they threw a metal object inside — a flare they said — and when Mom saw it she picked it up and threw it in the fireplace. The resounding explosion killed her young son and tore off her arm. The public considered it the ultimate gesture of harrassment. Mom said the boys weren't even home.

But the end was in sight for the James and Younger brothers. They made a fatal mistake when they decided to rob a bank in Northfield, Minnesota. When they came out they were cut down by armed citizens who were determined to kill as many of the outlaws as they could. Two of the outlaws were killed and the rest badly wounded. Those who hadn't been killed fled into a swamp, pursued by angry farmers.

The Younger brothers had all been wounded, and after they refused to abandon brother Jim, whose jaw had been shot away, the James brothers left them to fend for themselves. The Younger brothers were captured and sentenced to life in prison. The James brothers barely managed to escape.

Bob Younger died in prison, but thanks to the efforts of a lawyer whose life Cole had saved during the war, Cole and Jim were pardoned in 1901. Jim committed suicide in 1902. Cole lived the rest of his life quietly, and died in 1916 at the age of 72.

Routed by the unexpectedly fierce townsfolk, members of the James gang gallop about in confusion. Two lie dead, a third whose horse has been shot, runs for cover.

After Northfield, the James brothers went under false names to Nashville, Tennessee, intending to live quiet lives. But Jesse could never resist the temptation of a bank or a train with money in it, so three years later they robbed a train in Missouri. When they murdered two men a short time later, the Missouri governor put a price of $5,000 on each brother's head.

In 1882 Jesse James was shot dead in his home in St. Joseph by Robert Ford, a member of Jesse's gang who had succumbed to the lure of a big reward.

Ford was tried and sentenced to death for shooting an unarmed man, then rapidly pardoned by the governor. Ten years later Ford, reviled as a traitor, was shot by a man who lamented Jesse James' death.

As for Frank James, devotee of Shakespeare, six months after his brother's death he turned in his unloaded revolver to the governor. He was convicted of nothing. Minnesota wanted to try and convict him, but Minnesota was not allowed anywhere near him.

> "I have known no home. I have slept in all sorts of places. I have been charged with every great crime committed in Missouri or in her neighboring states. I am tired of this life of taut nerves...tired of the saddle, the revolver and the cartridge belt. I want to see if there is not some way out of it..."

Ford was nervous; he figured Jesse was on to him. "When Jesse took off his gun belt and stood on a chair to straighten a picture I knew it was my chance." He shot Jesse in the back of the head.

He lived quietly — dully, even — shooting off guns only as a starter at county fairs. He sold tickets to the "Home of the James" for fifty cents.

He died at the age of 75, thirty-two years after the State of Missouri had tried him for the murder of a passenger during one of his train robberies — tried him but let the Southern hero go free.

> Today, a delightful mix of truth and legend is kept alive at the James Farm, now owned by the county and restored by Friends of the James Farm, along with the cemetery where Jesse is buried and the bank in Liberty where his outlaw career got its start.

Frank James at home

Butch Cassidy
The Wild Bunch

Back row: Bill Carver and Kid Curry. Front row: Sundance Kid, Ben Kilpatrick, and Butch Cassidy.

They were the last of the old-time outlaw gangs that roared through the West in the late 1880s, flaunting the law and making life miserable for cattlemen, bankers, railroads, and the Pinkerton Agency.

It was a newspaper reporter who gave them the name Wild Bunch. The gang varied in numbers at times from a mere handful to a small army of outlaws. But there seems to have been a core group of about ten men who rode together. Others dropped out, were killed, or got the money they wanted and settled down to more responsible lives.

Undisputed leader of the Wild Bunch was Butch Cassidy.

Robert LeRoy Parker was his real name. He was the grandson of a respected Mormon who led the 1856 Hand Cart Expedition that firmly established the Mormon church in Utah. Apparently the tenets of the church never reached down to Robert LeRoy—though in truth it must be said that he made it a lifelong point to avoid needless violence. When pursued by posses, for instance, he always shot at the horses, never the riders. He once said, apparently truthfully, "I have never killed a man."

At seventeen he left home, changed his name to Cassidy, the name of a farmhand who had taught him how to shoot, and joined up with a gang led by Tom and Bill McCarty. From them he learned the robbery trade.

After participating in a couple of holdups, including the First National Bank of Denver, he apparently went straight for a while, working as an itinerant cowboy and living on the profits of his bank robbing endeavors.

14

But money doesn't last forever, and when next heard from he was arrested for stealing cattle. That unsuccessful caper cost him eighteen months in the Rawlins, Wyoming penitentiary–without chastening effect. When he got out, Cassidy formed his own gang.

Main headquarters of the Wild Bunch was Hole-in-the-Wall, a hiding place in a barren, desolate part of northern Wyoming–some of the most inaccessible country in the West. Once there had been a lake, but now it was a high plain shielded by sheer red cliffs. Because it had only one entrance and exit, it became a hideout for homeless, jobless cowhands, drifters, killers, and wanted men. Chief of this lawless bunch was "Kid Curry" Logan, a Montana fugitive who became Cassidy's second-in-command.

It was here at Hole-in-the-Wall, too, that Cassidy met Harry Longbaugh, the "Sundance Kid", who was to figure so prominently in his future.

Cassidy ran his gang democratically, asking the men's advice on various projects in progress. Aside from the way he made his living, he was a reasonably decent fellow. Even the WANTED posters described Cassidy as "cheery and affable."

But in the flair they displayed in action, the Wild Bunch lived up to their name–particularly after they turned their attention to trains.

They kept the Union Pacific's police detectives busy.

One thunderous train job took place at 2:30 a.m. on June 2, 1899, when the Wild Bunch used a red lantern to halt the Union Pacific's Overland Limited. In true, classical train robbery style, two men with guns climbed aboard and ordered the engineer to take the train across the bridge.

"Damned if I do!" he shouted.

His courage did him little good. One of the robbers knocked him unconscious and took over the throttle. The train slowly chugged across the bridge, which was immediately blown up by two other members of the band.

The four then went to the express car and shouted demands to Woodcock, the express messenger inside, to open the door. In a burst of bravery and devotion to his post, Woodcock replied, "Come in and get me!"

Cassidy slipped a stick of dynamite under the car and touched it off. The blast blew out one whole side of the car, and tossed Woodcock the entire length of the car, almost unconscious. Logan cocked his six-shooter at him. "Let him alone, Kid," Butch said. "A man with his nerve deserves not to be shot."

More dynamite blew the safe apart, sending a blizzard of currency wafting through the night air. The outlaws scooped up $30,000 of it, badly smeared with the remnants of a consignment of raspberries, and rode off with the sticky loot.

It wasn't the Wild Bunch's last encounter with Woodcock. The evening of August 29, 1900 they stopped the Union Pacific in Sweetwater Canyon. The scene and the players were the same. The outlaws demanded that the express messenger open the door. It was young Woodcock again.

Once more he refused to abandon his duty to protect the company funds. This time the conductor, who had seen the gang preparing a charge powerful enough to blow the car to bits, persuaded Woodcock to give up heroism and slide back the door.

For a while, Union Pacific was toying with the idea of paying off Cassidy with a pardon and an express guard position "at a good salary." Instead, they hired their own gang of gunfighters, outfitted them with rifles, and sent them out to bring in the Wild Bunch.

Cassidy could see the handwriting on the wall. The Glory days of the Old West were over. Barbed wire cut up the open range; the telegraph was everywhere to alert authorities. Railroads had a new strategy in which detectives loaded their horses aboard a special train to head off fleeing bandits trying to reach their hideouts.

Cassidy's new goal was the wild frontier of South America.

But first, to finance his new venture, Butch and Kid Curry led their raiders into Winnemucca, Nevada, to visit the First National Bank and make a withdrawal. While bank officials filled a wheat sack with $32,640 from the vault, a terrible odor filled the bank. Cassidy inched away from their accomplice, Bill Carver. "What happened to you?" he asked.

" I met a skunk along the way," an uneasy Carver explained.

Bank officials hurried them out.

Winnemucca, Nevada is rich cattle country, with immense ranches that stretch out across the desolate acreage. So it was not particularly noteworthy, one September day in 1900, when four drifting cowboys rode across the sagebrush and made camp on the edge of a ranch a few miles out of town.

It happened that this was a ranch that also raised mounts for the U.S. Cavalry, and the 10-year-old kid who lived there was allowed to ride any horse he chose.

But the horse the kid fell in love with was the powerful white horse that belonged to one of the cowboys encamped on the edge of the ranch. Each day he'd mount a different horse and ride out to see if the cowboy would trade.

The cowboy with the white horse was real friendly, but he wasn't interested in trading horses. What he wanted to hear about was the little town on the river, about the ranches around, who worked at the bank, and was the Sheriff always in town.

It was on the 19th day of September that Butch Cassidy, the Sundance Kid and Harvey Logan rode down into Winnemucca and robbed the First National Bank.

Tearing out of town on the gallop, the bandits emptied coin sacks through the town and out into the sagebrush to occupy the townspeople as they raced into the hills with only three pursuers on their trail. When the pursuers came bursting over a rise, they found themselves facing the gunbarrels of the robbers, now mounted on fresh horses and ready to ride.

Waving his gun in the air, Butch Cassidy called out, "You men better head back to town!" As the men reined around and left, Cassidy called after them, "Hey, tell the kid he can have the white horse."

The $32,640 stolen from the bank was never recovered. The Wild Bunch did remember the bank kindly, though. After they had their photograph taken in Fort Worth, Texas showing five members of the gang wearing new outfits bought with the money they had "withdrawn" from the bank, they sent a copy to the cashier,

Cassidy journeyed to New York sometime in late 1901, accompanied by his trusted confederate, Harry "Sundance Kid" Longbaugh and by Longbaugh's lady love, Etta Place. After taking in the city sights and stopping to have photographs taken, they sailed to Buenos Aires and new opportunities.

Sundance and Etta

The photo would eventually be circulated to almost every enforcement official in South America.

During the next decade, Butch, Sundance and Etta robbed banks and trains all across South America. Pinkerton men continued to keep track of them most of the time. One agent gave a clue to Cassidy's style of operating: "As soon as Cassidy entered an Indian village he would be playing with the children. After that, when hard pressed by authorities, he would always find a friendly hideout among the native population."

According to an official of the Concordia Tin Mines in Bolivia, Cassidy and Longbaugh worked for him off and on for several years, and had dinner with his family every Sunday. Occasionally they'd disappear for a few days, then come back to work. He never asked them where they'd been.

The last robbery Butch and Sundance pulled off was the Alpcoa Mine holdup. A mule train with the money from the mine was held up by the two outlaws on a jungle trail. But Butch reverted to his old cattle-thieving ways and appropriated a silver-gray mule of the mine superintendent. The hotel owner, who was also the local law official, spotted the stolen mule and rode ten miles to contact a small company of Bolivian cavalry.

Butch and Sundance were cooking meat on a beehive oven in the hotel patio when the soldiers rode up. Their captain ran into the patio shouting to the "Banditos Yanqui" to surrender. They were his last words. Sundance's bullet stopped him.

The outlaws escaped into their hut, but their guns were outside. The soldiers continued firing through the night, but there were no answering shots. At dawn the soldiers fired a few more rounds, and about ten o'clock they sent a woman carrying a baby to the hut. She came out crying, "The Banditos Yanqui are dead!"

Sundance had died of his wounds, Cassidy had killed himself during the night.

Etta was spared their miserable fate. Sometime earlier she had suffered an appendicitis attack and had to be taken to Denver.

Robert Redford as Sundance

Sam Brown
A Real Mean Man

It is said that the first thirty graves in the cemetery of Virginia City, Nevada were occupied by men killed in gunfights or cut down in saloon brawls. Sam Brown, a Texas bad man, took care of killing the first nine. And in the 53rd grave lies Sam Brown himself, killed by a Dutchman who didn't want to fight.

"Fighting Sam" Brown was considered the baddest of the bad in the Comstock silver mines of Virginia City. According to one contemporary account, "Most so-called desperados have some redeeming quality, the remembrance of which will cause a feeling of pity when they are gone. No such redeeming features shone in the character of Sam Brown, and no gleam of pity ever illuminated his pathway to the grave." The account goes on to regret that since Sam had never yet "killed any person who had friends with a special interest" no one had sought the help of the Vigilance Committee to dispose of him. In brief, Sam Brown had few friends.

Heavy set, with red hair and whiskers, he swaggered through the streets and barrooms, wearing a large revolver and a huge Bowie knife slung to his belt, insolent to anyone unarmed. When drunk, which was often, he was a cold-blooded killer. He was said to have added sixteen notches to the butt of his gun in 1860 alone.

It took a mild-mannered farmer, Henry Van Sickle, to put an end to his reign.

Sam's troubles began when he was called up as a witness at a trial of one of his young henchmen who was caught holding up a stage. He arrived in the courtroom fully prepared to bluster the judge and jury into intimidation and thereby free his cohort. Testimony had been going against the robber, so when it came time for Sam to testify he was boiling mad, fully fortified with liquor, and prepared to bluster the district attorney into submission. The edge of his resolution was considerably dulled when he found himself facing the muzzle of a gun held in the hand of attorney Bill Stewart, who would one day be the U.S. Senator from Nevada. Sam's weakened testimony did nothing to save his fellow hoodlum.

So it was that he arrived at a roadside inn raging at his failure and ready to take it out on anyone in his way. That someone was an innocent Dutch farmer named Henry Van Sickle. After a few wild shots at the unarmed man, Sam rode off. Now the placid farmer had his dander up. A chase ensued. Van Sickle left the road to "head him off at the pass," and Sam walked into the trap. Van Sickle shot him dead.

A coroner's jury held that "Brown came to his end by the dispensation of a Divine Providence." And despite the fact that it was Sam's thirtieth birthday, the jury announced, "It served him right."

Tom Bell
Double Trouble

Oh, what was your name in the States?
Was it Thompson, or Johnson or Bates?
Did you flee for your life,
Or murder your wife?
Say, what was your name in the States?

In California's gold mining region, '49ers seldom were called by their real names, but were nicknamed Red, or Slim, or Dutch Jake. It was not always healthy or polite to inquire too closely into a man's background unless he volunteered it.

Thus, when a man named Dr. Thomas Hodges gave up doctoring and turned to grand larceny for his support, he saw no reason to give prison officials his own name. Recalling a small-time bandit he had heard of, he appropriated that man's name and entered prison as Tom Bell.

Hodges-Bell didn't linger long in prison. Feigning serious illness (and he did know how to do that), he managed to get more freedom than other prisoners, which he soon expanded by bribing prison guards to leave a gate unlocked, thus securing for himself complete freedom.

Unleashed into the outside world, he joined forces with an unsavory companion with whom he left prison, and embarked on a new career of serious crime. In so doing, he perpetrated a puzzle that had both sheriffs and citizens baffled for years.

On the one hand, there was a Tom Bell described as a ferocious fellow, ready to shot on sight, showing victims no mercy. According to one newspaper report, the man "carried six revolvers and wears a breastplate of thin iron around his body."

No sooner was this swashbuckling Tom Bell fixed in authorities' minds than a conflicting image of the man appeared. Tom Bell was no fierce fellow bristling with weapons. Indeed, his most notable characteristic was his gentle nature. In one instance quoted, when his partner in crime had found it necessary to wound a traveler who had shown a disposition to protect his moneybelt, Tom had bound up the bullet hole, halted a wagon and asked the driver to take the injured man to a doctor.

Some who knew Tom Bell reported him to be a small, inoffensive specimen who had failed at mining and thus turned to robbery and horse-stealing.

Not until tall, gaunt Tom Bell, the gang leader, highwayman and killer, was finally caught did the jumble get untangled. There were two Tom Bells.

"Throw down the box!"

In reality, Dr. Hodges had not always been a bad sort. In his home town in Tennessee he was well regarded. He served in the Mexican war as a doctor/soldier; when it ended he headed for California and joined other prospectors looking for gold. When that didn't prove profitable he drifted into bad ways.

Whatever other qualifications he may have had in his new career, he was cursed with one identifying mark that was to be his undoing. His nose! Once straight and handsome, it had been smashed flat at the bridge in some violent episode of his past and reduced to a mere button.

Throughout 1856 this Tom Bell swaggered through the gold country, preying on everyone as he went. In the heat of mid-August, his gang decided to go big and waylay the Wells Fargo stage between Marysville and Camptonville.

One of Bell's scouts, dressed in miner's garb and posing as an ordinary passenger, got off the stage at the California House stop and waved it on, then rushed inside to pass the word that the treasure box under the driver's seat was loaded with no less than $100,000 in gold dust.

Having performed his part in the caper, he settled down for a drink while Bell and his men, armed to the teeth, took off after the stage.

Heading down a little-known short cut trail, they overtook the stage, faced the driver and made the familiar request, "Throw down the box!" Bill Dobson, who was riding shotgun beside the driver, showed fight. With five armed men facing him, he fired his shotgun point-blank and calmly proceeded to draw his Colts. More than forty shots were exchanged. One of the most heroic fights in the history of California staging was on.

By the time the bandits were driven off, one passenger was dead, two wounded, and the driver had a flesh wound in his forearm. But he succeeded in driving the coach to Marysville, where a madly cheering crowd made him the hero of the hour.

The Sheriff's posses went into action, and one after another, all members of Bell's gang were gathered in. Bell himself escaped capture for another ten months. He was picked up by the Sheriff of Calaveras County. With that nose, he couldn't hide his identity.

There was no trial. The Sheriff of Calaveras County decided that. Hodges, alias Tom Bell, was given four hours to write farewell letters to his folks back in Tennessee. At the end of that time he was left hanging by a rope from the branch of a convenient tree, while the posse slowly descended through the ravine where he had been trapped, bearing the letters the men had promised to mail to Tennessee.

Rattlesnake Dick
Crimes in the Mines

Compared with more grandiose schemes of crime, Rattlesnake Dick was pretty small potatoes. In retrospect, perhaps the most striking thing about him was that name

Dick Barter and two brothers, sons of a British army officer in Canada, arrived in the gold mines of northern California in 1850 — a trifle late, perhaps, for the best diggins. They settled in a mining camp called Rattlesnake Bar, awash in enthusiasm and high spirits.

It soon became apparent, though, that it takes a lot of hard labor to make "easy pickings," and the two older brothers decided to give up. Dick stayed. He refused to accept claims that the area had "placered out;" in fact, he kept up a level of enthusiasm that became a standing joke among older miners. Not in malice, but in jest, they began calling him "Rattlesnake Dick."

It's hard to say what went wrong with Dick's life. He worked hard, was able and clever. But somehow he earned the ill will of one of the miners. When the proprietor of the small store thought someone was stealing his stock, a man who hated Dick reported he was the thief. He was arrested and tried, but found not guilty. It was only the beginning.

Later the same year, a Mormon named Crow missed his mule and declared flatly that Dick had stolen it. This time Dick was convicted. But before they had a chance to haul him off to prison, the mule was found and the man who had stolen it confessed to the crime.

Determined to start a new life, he left for Shasta, took the name Dick Woods, and set about to live an upright life as a miner. Then one day some travelers from the old diggins came to Shasta, spotted him, and started spreading the word that he was a bad sort.

Driven to the wall, Dick turned to a life of crime. On his first holdup, he told his victim, "If anyone asks who robbed you, tell them it was Rattlesnake Dick!" And thus his name was spread.

It was mostly small stuff: robbing sluice-boxes, robbing on the highroad, running off a horse or two. But in time he teamed up with some serious highwaymen on a project to assume ownership of some gold bullion being shipped by Wells-Fargo on muleback from Yreka.

The mule trains were usually guarded by a convoy, but that wasn't the problem. A few well-armed men should be able to surprise the guards, tie them up, and make off with the treasure. The hitch lay in the fact that the mules all bore the express company's brand and would be recognized anywhere.

But Dick had a plan. While four of the gang took care of the robbery, Dick and a cohort would be down in Auburn stealing mules from a corral he knew, then meet the others at a designated hideaway to transfer the loot from the mules branded W-F.

The holdup went off without a hitch — but Dick was late for his appointment. In fact, he never did show up because he was in jail. His companions, unable to carry the entire heavy load on their horses, buried half of it somewhere near Shasta. The man who did the burying was killed, and the bullion has never been found.

Dick was never convicted of complicity on the holdup. But his life wasn't worth much after that. He continued to engage in petty thievery, was often caught and put in jail. But no jail could hold him. He always escaped, always on the run.

His luck ran out one night when he was riding on horseback with a companion, a mile out of Auburn. Two men rode up behind them and called on the riders to halt. Dick fired, killing one pursuer and shattering the left hand of the other. Still, the injured one fired twice. Dick swayed in his saddle, then rose and spurred his horse down the road, his companion after him.

The next morning the body of Rattlesnake Dick was found beside the road a mile away, very dead indeed. Two bullets had passed through his body, but there was a third that puzzled authorities, a bullet to the brain. Had he committed suicide? Did his companion finish him off?

The mystery was never solved. But one reporter stated flatly that by Dick's side, when he was found, there had been a scrap of paper on which was scrawled with pencil, "I die as all true Britons do!"

Joaquin Murietta
The Mexican Bandito

Most romantic of Gold Country bandits was the legendary Joaquin Murieta, who seemed to be everywhere at once—sometimes all on the same day.

Immortalized in books, paintings and even a Hollywood motion picture, Murieta is said to have endured endless racial persecution. He swore vengeance on his alleged Yankee persecutors after they tied him to a tree, beat him bloody, then ravished his wife and murdered his brother.

This legend appears to have little foundation, and has been severely challenged by historians, who contend there was no way one bandit could be so many places at one time, and that every bad man named either Joaquin or Murieta got credit for being Joaquin Murieta.

Nevertheless, the legend of the flamboyant bandit lived long with old-timers who retold for years about his courage in ordering a bullet-proof vest to be made, which he tested by shooting himself at point-blank range.

At Hornitos, a mining camp once heavily populated by Mexican miners, there is an underground tunnel said to have been used by the bandit to escape hotly-pursuing lawmen. In the village of Volcano there used to be a well-disguised treehouse where Joaquin is said to have hidden while puzzled rangers milled around beneath him.

Whoever he was, or whoever they were, legend has it that Murieta died in a blaze of glory, hunted down and shot to death by a lawman named Harry Love.

In this there is considerable truth.

Henry Love was a mean, ugly and murderous bounty hunter who determined to capitalize on the outrage of citizens at the explosion of banditry in early 1853, largely by dispossessed Mexicans. Five outlaws were identified, at first only by Christian name which (curiously) all of them shared—Joaquin. Love came upon them one night around a campfire. He opened fire, killing several, among them a man that the gang named as Joaquin Valenzuela.

Whoever he was, Love cut off the head of the leader who, he insisted, was Murieta. Preserving it for identification in a keg of brandy, he collected the reward offered by the Governor—$1,000. Later he received another sum, $5,000, from a grateful California legislature.

Newspaper sketch "drawn directly from the head-in-alcohol"

To further increase his profitability, he exhibited the head, along with another prize, the hand of a bandit known as Three Fingered Jack, around the state.

EXHIBITED
FOR ONE DAY ONLY!
AT THE STOCKTON HOUSE!
THIS DAY, AUG. 12, FROM 9 A. M., UNTIL 6, P. M.
THE HEAD
Of the renowned Bandit!
JOAQUIN!
AND THE
HAND OF THREE FINGERED JACK!

23

Black Bart
The Gentleman Bandit

He was the man Wells Fargo wanted most. The reward they offered for his capture exceeded the total of the amounts he got away from them.

Gallant and polite, eminently respectable-appearing in his bowler hat and satin-faced Chesterfield, the man who called himself by the fearsome name of Black Bart was a notorious highwayman who terrorized stagecoach drivers and gave Wells Fargo detectives a bad time for eight years. Yet he never fired a shot.

In actual fact the most mild-mannered of men, Black Bart was, without any doubt, the most famous of all stagecoach robbers, credited with 28 robberies between 1877 and 1883. Stagecoach drivers throughout northern California lived in dread of the day when he would step out from behind the brush in some secluded ravine and call out politely, "Will you please throw down your treasure box, sir?"

Here was no rumpled desperado galloping up to the stagecoach in a cloud of dust. Bart was always on foot, carrying only a shotgun and a blanket roll in which he had tucked an old axe with which to break open the strongbox. His working clothes were unique. He dressed in a long linen duster and wore a flour sack over his head, with holes cut out for the eyes.

His locations were chosen carefully, always at sharp bends in the road where the horses would be moving at a walk. Bart launched his robberies in classic fashion. Stepping from the brush alongside some lonely road, he pointed a very large shotgun at the drivers. As they sawed their teams to a halt, he alleviated his concern for his own flesh by taking advantage of the drivers' concern for their horseflesh. He sheltered himself from gunfire by standing as close as he could get to the heads of the horses.

Bart was gentle with his victims and never harmed driver or passengers. He had style. He had wit and charm. Newspaper accounts of the day hailed him as a man who "takes only from the rich and spares all life." It was revealed later that he never owned a single shell for his shotgun and could not have fired it even in self-defense.

His first known crime occurred on July 26, 1875, when he stopped the Sonora-Milton express coach four miles east of Copperopolis in California's gold country.

John Shine, the startled driver, at first busied himself following orders, then hesitated. A deep voice roared from the flour-sack mask, directed at the bandit's "confederates" stationed at strategic positions on a hillside covered with high manzanita brush. "Boys, stay where you are!" he directed them. "If he dares to shoot, give him a solid volley!"

It was only after the bandit had looted the strong box and hiked off across the rugged hills that Shine discovered he had been hoodwinked. Going back to pick up the emptied box, he could see the highwayman's confederates still had their rifles leveled at him. Still, he gingerly approached the brush—only to find that the guns were sticks fastened in place.

But it was neither trickery nor ferocity that turned Black Bart into a lasting legend.

On his fourth robbery he launched a habit that thereafter provided newspapers with thousands of column-inches of copy and engaged the fascinated attention of readers for years—making Black Bart a celebrity in his own time.

On August 3, 1877, Bart was successful in holding up the Wells Fargo stage between Fort Ross and the Russian River. Authorities who arrived on the scene to investigate found a battered-open strongbox on the ground with the following message pinned to it:

I've labored long and hard for bread,
For honor and for riches,
But on my corns too long you've tred,
You fine-haired sons of bitches . . .

It was signed Black Bart, Po 8 (po-ate).

The doggerel verse and humorous signature captivated both newspaper editors and the public. And if Wells Fargo considered him a downright nuisance, the foppish bandit acquired a certain fame for his charm and wit. It was unquestionably wrong of him to take the money in the strongbox, but on one thing he was adamant—he never robbed the passengers. On one occasion, three frightened ladies offered him their money and jewelry. "Don't be alarmed, ladies," he told them with a courtly bow, "I wouldn't harm a hair on your heads."

This colorful career came to an end when Bart was wounded while escaping from a holdup near Copperopolis—ironically, at almost the exact spot where he had held up his first stage more than eight years earlier. It was the largest heist he had ever accomplished—some $4,900 in gold and coins. He was hammering open the lockbox when the driver started taking potshots at him with a rifle owned by a young hunter passenger. Bart grabbed the lockbox

and darted into the brush, but he left behind something more serious than the loot. He dropped several pieces of evidence, the most serious being a silk handkerchief that was the key to his capture. On it was a laundry mark, FX-0.7. The Wells Fargo detectives spent eight days checking San Francisco laundries, and finally traced it to a customer who claimed to be a mining engineer. He turned out to be Charles E. Bolton, one of San Francisco's leading citizens and a man who had connections in the police department.

After his arrest, Bolton confessed to the crimes of Black Bart and told a strange tale of his life.

He was born Charles Boles and grew up in Illinois as an intelligent, well-educated citizen. After serving in the Civil Way, he followed the crowd to the California Gold Rush. That didn't work out, so he went to work clerking in several stage offices, where he studied shipments and schedules. When he decided to make his move, his prior knowledge made the job easy.

Everything went so well, he tried it again. And again. With success came prosperity. Boles moved to San Francisco, changed his name to Charles Bolton, where he moved in prominent social circles, always nattily dressed. His reputation was of a non-smoking, non-drinking, God-fearing man with business interests in the mines. It was so easy. Whenever he needed more cash, he had only to put away his derby and pack up his linen duster.

Justice was swift. On November 17, 1883—five days after his arrest and two weeks after his last fateful robbery—Black Bart was sentenced to six years in prison. Two days later, he was behind the walls of San Quentin.

After his release, Bart hung about San Francisco, then drifted south to the San Joaquin Valley. He then disappeared, leaving a valise in his lodgings. He was never heard from again. He simply vanished from the face of the earth.

There were rumors, of course. He had been seen in Kansas, Mexico, Japan. A story circulated that a New York paper had carried his obituary. One story claimed that Wells Fargo had pensioned him off and sent him away.

The fact is, no one will ever know for sure just what happened to Black Bart, the most famous stage robber of them all.

A MESSAGE FROM BART

*Here I lay me down to sleep
To wait the coming morrow,
Perhaps success, perhaps defeat
And everlasting sorrow,
Yet come what will, I'll try it once,
My condition can't be worse,
And if there's money in that box,
'Tis munney in my purse.*

☞ Agents of W., F. & Co will **not** post this circular, but place them in the hands of your local and county officers, and reliable citizens in your region. Officers and citizens receiving them are respectfully requested to preserve them for future reference.

Agents WILL PRESERVE a copy on file in their office.

$800.00 Reward!
ARREST STAGE ROBBER!

On the 3d of August, 1877, the stage from Fort Ross to Russian River was stopped by one man, who took from the Express box about $300, coin, and a check for $305.52, on Grangers' Bank of San Francisco, in favor of Fisk Bros. The Mail was also robbed. On one of the Way Bills left with the box the Robber wrote as follows:—

"I've labored long and hard for bread—
For honor and for riches—
But on my corns too long you've trod,
You fine haired sons of bitches.
BLACK BART, the P o 8.

Driver, give my respects to our friend, the other driver; but I really had a notion to hang my old disguise hat on his weather eye." *(fac simile.)*

Respectfully
B·B

It is believed that he went to the Town of Guerneville about daylight next morning.

The Sperry Hotel (now Murphy Hotel)

Evening the Odds

On an evening in February 1880, a man who had registered at the Sperry Hotel in Murphys, California as Carlos Bolton, was invited by two fellow guests to join them in a friendly game of poker. Although the two men had the unmistakable appearance of experienced gamblers, the quiet, scholarly Mr. Bolton agreed. After dinner they assembled at the bar, stakes were agreed upon, and the cards were cut.

As the hours passed, it became quite apparent that Mr. Bolton and a fourth guest had more than met their match in the gentlemen from San Francisco, whose winnings made an impressive stack of gold and currency. The fact that the dealer's hands were exceedingly nimble with the cards did not escape Mr. Bolton's notice.

Finally, Bolton remarked that inasmuch as his capital was at low ebb and he had to arise at an early hour, he felt it was time to retire. The others agreed, and bidding one another goodnight, went to their rooms.

The following morning the peace and quiet of the hostelry was suddenly shattered as the guest named Wheeler burst from his room hollering for the proprietor. In one hand he furiously waved a piece a note paper, in the other he brandished a gun. He demanded to see Mr. Bolton at once, but was told that the gentleman in question had saddled his horse and left at daybreak.

At last the proprietor managed to take the note from Wheeler, and the corners of his mouth twitched in a suppressed smile as he read the message.

"My dear Sir: May I take this opportunity to express my appreciation for an edifying evening in your company.

"I found your demonstration of the 'hand being quicker than the eye' most illuminating. But may I humbly suggest, Dear Sir, that when dealing from the bottom of the deck, it is unfortunate to be so placed at a table that a mirror, close by, reveals what is going on behind the scenes.

"In view of the circumstances I feel called upon, at the completion of this missive, to enter your room and relieve you of this evening's ill-gotten gains, together with such other trinkets of value as you may possess. In doing this, I take pleasure in returning the compliment by demonstrating, successfully I hope, that 'the footstep is quicker than the ear.'

"Not wishing to completely embarrass you, I shall leave enough funds to cover your obligations incurred while staying at this hotel.

"Believe me, Dear Sir, to be Faithfully Yours, BLACK BART."

The Dalton Boys
A Sorry End

There were fifteen Dalton children in all, ten of them sons. Father of the clan was a ne'er-do-well saloon-keeper. When his wife insisted, on moral principles, that he give up the whiskey business, he sold it and took up the life of an itinerant horse trader, home just often enough to sire another Dalton.

For the family, it was a hand-to-mouth existence, but Mother Dalton ruled her small army with a firm hand and an iron will. She didn't want them to turn out like her brother's boys, the Youngers.

When the oldest boys were teen-agers, she decided to better their lot and take up a homestead in Indian Territory, near the town of Coffeyville, Kansas. It was here that three of her sons were to come to grief.

Emmet got work on a ranch, where he met some of the bad company that would eventually shorten his life. Later he joined his brothers, Grat and Bob, as deputies for "Hanging Judge" Parker, patrolling Indian Territory. The pay wasn't much, but they picked up a little extra cash on the side as part-time rustlers.

Then they decided on a little train robbery. It was not a lucky venture. The fireman was killed, the Wells Fargo messenger wounded. Grat was arrested and tried in the profitless stick-up. He drew a twenty-year sentence, but escaped. Bob, who was also wanted, got away.

Presently Mother Dalton's three bad boys were reunited in their Oklahoma sod hutch, their feet solidly set on the outlaw path. Bob, in his early twenties, was the leader. Besides Grat, his older brother, and 20-year-old Emmet, Bob could call on the services of seven other badmen, the friends Emmet had made on the ranch. They kept up a busy schedule for the next year, hitting on trains and escaping from posses.

The Daltons would have been just another band of train robbers in frontier history had it not been for their reckless and bloody raid on the banks in Coffeyville—one of the most idiotic ventures in outlaw history. Not only were they known to the citizens of the town, their wanted posters had been posted throughout the area.

Five horsemen rode into Coffeyville that fateful morning in October. The town was just beginning to stir as they jogged toward the sunny plaza. Here they met their first surprise.

Workmen were tearing up the street for repairs, and the hitching rack near the bank was torn down. They should have known that in advance. Bob swallowed his dismay and directed his band into the alley a block away.

Wearing false beards, they entered the bank. Then more bad luck. The newspaper editor, who just happened to be passing, looked into the plate glass window and saw a Winchester raised toward the cashier's counter, and he could recognize Grat Dalton in spite of the false beard. "The bank's being robbed!" he called out. Others heard it and picked up the cry.

Inside the bank, things weren't going well at all.

"It's a time lock," the cashier lied, "won't open till 9:45." It was then 9:42. "I'll wait," said the oldest Dalton, as nervy as the cashier. At that moment, gunfire began to sound in the Plaza. The next three minutes would be crucial.

Meanwhile, across the street, Bob Dalton was robbing the First National, where things were going smoother. They were about to leave with a grain sack filled with $21,000, but by now gunfire in the plaza was so heavy Bob decided to go the back way, although it meant an extra block to get to the horses. Handing the sack to his confederate, he took aim at a young man pursuing them, the first casualty of the West's deadliest battle. Then he picked off two men who owned a boot shop where the Dalton youngsters had always bought their shoes. The next two shots took down two merchants; the bank cashier dropped next.

Bob got to the alley the same time as Grat, who was clutching a paltry $1,500 swept from the counter drawer. In the next three minutes, "Blood Alley" got its name. The two confederates were hit. Then Bob. Then Emmet was hit, twice. Grat fell dead.

Emmet, bleeding profusely but still clutching the sack of $21,000, might have escaped if he had bolted. Instead, the 20-year-old outlaw forced his horse to the side of the brother he worshiped, and reached down to lift his dying brother. He fell with eighteen buckshot in his back, just as Bob breathed his last.

Only fifteen minutes had passed since the five bandits had tied their mounts to the fence in the alley.

DALTONS!

The Robber Gang Meet Their Waterloo in Coffeyville.

A Desperate Attempt to Rob Two Banks

From the *Coffeyville Journal* October 7, 1892.

"Strong men wept great tears of grief, whilst the women and children cried in agony," reported the town's newspaper.

It was really the end of the desperado legions that had terrorized the frontier towns. Law and order were taking hold, but the Daltons wouldn't believe it.

Emmet, the only one to survive the raid, wasn't in any shape to stand trial for five months. He pleaded guilty to second-degree murder and was sentenced to a life term in the Kansas State Penitentiary. He had just turned 21.

The Emmet who came out fifteen years later, pardoned by the governor, bore little resemblance to the wild youth who had followed his big brothers into a life of crime with such eagerness. The man who emerged was a churchgoer, a crusader against crime.

Doctors were still digging shot out of his frame thirty years after Coffeyville, but Emmet was thriving in a new life as a building contractor in Los Angeles. He also dabbled in real estate, wrote movie scenarios, even acted some bit parts in crime-doesn't-pay films himself.

Just once he went back to Coffeyville. Standing in the cemetery where his brothers were buried, and looking down on their graves, he told a reporter, "I challenge the world to produce the history of an outlaw who ever got anything out of it but that."

Jesse James had ridden roughshod over the West for sixteen years. Cole, Bob and Jim Younger, the Daltons' celebrated cousins, had terrorized banks for a decade before they were cut down by gunfire. The reign of the Dalton boys was brief. Their escapades spanned only eighteen months.

29

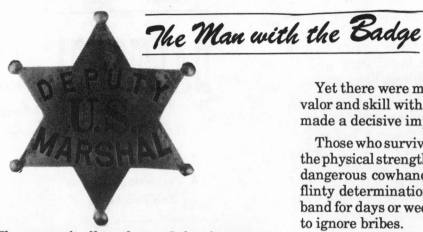

They weren't all good men. It has long since been recognized, even in the most sanguine portrayal of early-day lawmen, that the man with the star gleaming on his vest was not always what he should have been. Like Wyatt Earp, they occasionally had a tendency to wander somewhat loosely from one side of the law to the other.

The guardian of law and order with a second career as a practicing outlaw might one day be lynched by the very people whose lives he was sworn to protect—and whose cattle he had been stealing. A Wyoming sheriff—he had once ridden with Billy the Kid—did such a remarkable job of cleaning up the county that grateful citizens gave him a fancy engraved gun. Inexplicably, he used it to hold up a bank.

Yet there were many who did indeed display valor and skill with a gun, and collectively they made a decisive impact on frontier justice.

Those who survived were fast with a gun, had the physical strength to control mobs of drunken, dangerous cowhands in from a drive, had the flinty determination to trail a killer or outlaw band for days or weeks, and the moral integrity to ignore bribes.

Their dedication was often impressive. Colorado's Sheriff Charles Neiman, beaten unconscious by a pair of mean and dangerous rustlers, got to his feet and saddled up. Battered and groggy, he trailed the pair along the road to Steamboat Springs, caught a stage so he could head off the fugitives before they could reach the railroad. Two miles short of Steamboat, the fugitives hailed the stage and stepped inside to face Neiman's cocked gun. "Good morning, gentlemen," the sheriff said with a grim smile, "Breakfast is waiting for you back at the jail."

Most of the cowtowns or mining towns of the West were grateful to find someone brave enough to strap on his six-shooters and maintain some semblance of law and order. Should it be an upright but ineffectual fellow townsman? Or a newcomer of dubious past but iron nerve? Ineptitude seldom won out. Few citizens worried how the man had erred in the past. They wanted the man best equipped to deal with his own kind.

Cowboys "hurrahing" a town
By Frederic Remington

The marshal had a multitude of mundane duties besides showdowns and shoot-outs. In Abilene, Wild Bill Hickok kept the streets cleared of litter as well as riotous cowboys. Half Virgil Earp's arrests were for disturbing the peace. Marshals served subpoenas, kept records, and presided over the jail, which was usually a one-room shack, so flimsy that a gang of rowdies could kick it apart to free a friend.

Still, the marshal's gun had to be ready and swift at all times, for the frontier town was a tinderbox simply waiting for a drunken brawl to ignite a tragedy.

In the peace-keeping hierarchy, county sheriffs were a cut above town marshals. The job of county sheriff could be profitable, since much of the time was spent collecting county taxes, of which the collector received a percentage.

There was a third level of lawman, the United States marshal. He was charged with enforcing federal law, but often held additional commissions so he could work at the local level.

There were other lawmen who worked for railroads, express companies, the Cattlemen's Association, and private detective organizations. Among the best of the detectives was William Pinkerton, who directed a small army of operators on the frontier.

Train guards carried an arsenal in their head-end cars.

The Pinkertons had the first outlaw rogues' gallery. The iron rule, followed by all detectives, was to get pictures of the criminals they caught or chased, and then a list of their aliases, nicknames, hangouts and method of operation. As the years went on, it developed into a rather thorough and dependable "Index of Outlaws." In the Pinkerton files today is the original photo of the Wild Bunch, taken in a Texas studio, which was tracked down by a Pinkerton detective who blanketed the West with copies. In some aspects, Pinkerton was the forerunner of the FBI.

The tools of the western lawman were few. He supplied his own rifle, six-shooter and ammunition, a horse, slicker and blanket. The town provided the jail, courts, judges and juries.

The lawman always lived close to death and violence. One of the best was Bill Tilghman, once marshal of Dodge City—an intelligent, resourceful and persistent lawman who chased down the Doolin Gang, the Daltons, and the Starr Gang, contributing to the demise of all three.

Ironically, "Uncle Billy" Tilghman survived gunfights, ambushes and countless manhunts for the most dangerous men in the Wild West—only to be killed by a drunken Prohibition agent.

Pinkerton and two well-armed agents

31

Bat Masterson

The Jaunty Lawman

It happened in Dodge City, Kansas. A stranger in town asked a resident where he could find Bat Masterson. A lawyer who overheard the question broke in and said: "Look for one of the most perfectly made men you ever saw, a well-dressed, good-looking fellow, and when you see such a man call him 'Bat' and you have hit the bull's-eye."

While the picture of a natty sheriff in a derby hat, wearing a jaunty smile while dispatching his enemies with a whack of his gold- headed cane, is fairly accurate, it tends to obscure the fascinating story of a young lawman who helped tame the toughest cowtown in the West with courage, humor, even compassion—plus his skill with a gun.

In all, there were five Masterson brothers who grew up on a homestead near Wichita. The two youngest boys never had any particular claim to fame. But Ed, the eldest, eventually became the marshal of Dodge City; Bartholomew, the second-born, called "Bat" for short, served as the sheriff of Ford County, which had Dodge City as its county seat; and Jim, the third brother, followed Ed as Dodge's marshal. But Bat was always the daring one, the maker of big plans.

When he was 19, Bat talked his two brothers into leaving the boring life of the farm to go buffalo hunting in southwestern Kansas. Ed and Jim returned to the farm after a while, but Bat just kept moving, meeting adventures enough to satisfy the most foolhardy of farm boys.

In the Texas Panhandle town of Adobe Walls (three stores and a saloon) he joined with a company of 35 hunters in holding off a determined attack by 500 Indian warriors who were spreading havoc in the region.

In Sweetwater, Texas he had his first real gunfight. The details are somewhat obscure, but what seems certain is that Bat took a fancy to the sweetheart of an army sergeant named Melvin King. When King found them together one night in a saloon, he opened fire on Bat. The girl threw herself in front of Bat and was killed instantly. The bullet which passed through her body lodged in Bat's pelvis, but as he fell, with the sergeant cocking his pistol for another shot, Bat fired back. King died the next day. As for Bat, he sustained a limp and took to carrying a cane—at first out of necessity, later for adornment alone.

When Bat arrived in Dodge City, he was 23, strikingly handsome with his mop of black hair, slate-blue eyes and compact body, and something of a dandy, wearing a sombrero, Mexican sash, and two gleaming silver-plated six-shooters in silver studded holsters—a get-up he soon abandoned.

His brothers, Ed and Jim, had already arrived in Dodge, and were nicely settled in. Jim was part owner of a saloon-dance hall, and Ed—the steady-going eldest brother—had just been appointed assistant marshal of Dodge.

Neither Ed nor Bat knew much about the business of being a lawman, but within six months both had been elevated to powerful positions. Ed, then 25, got promoted to marshal. Bat, a year younger, was elected sheriff of Ford County.

They both had a lot to learn. But Ed, at least, had some months to get used to the job. Nothing is less lively than a cattle town in winter; there would be little to do until summer when the cowboys roared into town, raising hell.

Dodge City 1878: Not much of a town, but when the cowboys came in off the trail it was a real hell- raiser.

As for Bat, he was a quick learner. He started by discarding the sombrero in favor of a smart bowler hat worn at a rakish tilt, and wearing a tailor-made black suit as he made his rounds in a buggy and team.

Two weeks into his term of office, he had a chance to launch himself in a blaze of glory.

Six bandits had been foiled in a train robbery 35 miles out of Dodge, and were fleeing loose. Two groups of pursuers had taken chase but never got near the bandits.

Anticipating the bandits' movements, Bat led a posse through a driving blizzard to an abandoned camp where he calculated they'd seek shelter from the storm. Bat sent one man out as a decoy to lure them into camp. Before the fugitives could brush the snow from their coats, the sheriff sprang forward, his two six-shooters cocked, and ordered them to throw up their hands.

The other four bandits were still on the loose, but a month later two of them showed up in Dodge. Bat summoned his brother Ed and took the outlaws without a gunfight. The fifth bandit eluded capture for half a year more, and the sixth was never caught. But Bat's triumph was splendid enough.

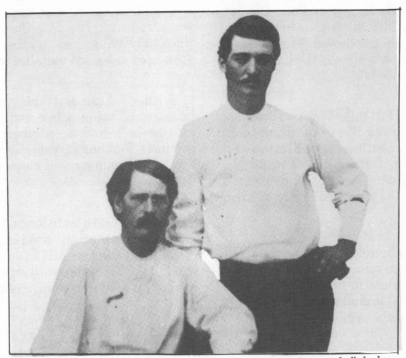

Wyatt and Bat together in Dodge. The scroll on Earp's shirt is his marshal's badge.

For Bat Masterson, it was clear sailing from then on. The dapper young lawman became a familiar sight as he whipped his team and buggy around his bailiwick—an enormous area stretching 100 miles east-west, 75 miles north-south. Outlaws wisely began to give this new hard-working sheriff a wide berth, and the plains of Ford County were at relative peace.

Ed's job, on the other hand, was becoming increasingly heavy. And unlike Bat, he never liked to use a gun, preferring to talk his adversaries into submission. Bat worried that his brother's inborn gentleness and easy-going manner would never inspire fear among the low element he had to deal with.

For a peace officer, establishing respect for authority could be a matter of life and death. Bat rarely had to fire his revolvers, for the simple reason that most of his adversaries didn't dare shoot it out with him. He maintained his reputation by spending endless hours practicing, shooting at empty cans. Bat once told a reporter, in retrospect, "We used to file the notch of the hammer till the trigger would 'pull sweet,' which is another way of saying that the blamed gun would pretty near go off if you looked at it."

Some historians believe that the only killing that could be actually attributed directly to Bat was Sergeant King, the scorned lover in Sweetwater.

Ed had the respect of the citizenry, and it certainly took courage to face drunken cowboys, con men, and restless soldiers from Fort Dodge without the support of a six-shooter. But one night, while trying to disarm a couple of rowdies, he found himself in real trouble. Both men pulled their guns, Ed nailed one of them to the wall, but was in danger from the other. From across the street Bat saw what was happening and fired at the second man. Ed, not knowing who was shooting, drew his gun, allowing the freed cowboy to get out his six-shooter. Ed stumbled to the ground, mortally wounded, shot at such close range that his coat caught fire.

The next day every business in town closed, for everyone loved the young, gentle sheriff who hated to use a gun.

A year later, it was another Masterson, Jim, who took his brother's place as sheriff of Dodge. On the same day he took office, Bat was defeated for re-election as county sheriff.

So Bat was on the move again, restless and footloose, a familiar face in the gambling halls of Denver and Trinidad, Leadville and Tombstone.

Now there were streaks of gray in his dark hair. He was heavier, wore a drooping mustache, a black derby, and in winter a sealskin-trimmed chinchilla ulster that reached almost to the tops of his patent-leather shoes.

Once, when his brother Jim got into a shooting scrape, Bat came to his rescue, all the way from New Mexico. He got off the train, spotted the ruffians who were giving his brother trouble, and called out to them, "I have come over a thousand miles to settle this; I know you are heeled, now fight!" The shooting lasted three minutes, with Bat sheltered behind an embankment. One bullet came so close it sprayed dirt at his face. The ruffians were routed, Bat paid a $10 fine for carrying a gun, and left town the same night he arrived.

He continued flitting from one boomtown to another. In Denver he bought out his favorite theater, the Palace Variety Theater. Denver was an important stopover for Broadway variety productions, and many beautiful women passed through the Palace. But only one captivated him—the petite, blond Emma Walters, a singer and dancer. After a short courtship, Bat married her.

He had also become a pugilistic expert, acting as referee and putting together heavyweight fights. He bought a saloon in a miserable Colorado town called Creede, where he patrolled his premises in a lavender corduroy suit. During this period he met William Lewis, a correspondent for the New York Sun—a man who would help shape Bat Masterson's future.

Bat was now a national celebrity, but he had unbuckled his gun belt for good. His reflexes slowed, his eyes dimmed. He left Colorado and the West for good and landed—of all places—in New York City, earning his living as a sports writer.

And he met President Theodore Roosevelt.

Teddy Roosevelt never forgot the West. His valued friends were cowboys, hunters, sheriffs, ranchers, painters, and writers of the Old West. But incredibly, the favorite of the 26th president of the United States was a gunfighter, gambler, saloon and dance-hall owner, fight promoter, and New York sports columnist— Bat Masterson.

Their friendship lasted for years, with Bat always a welcome guest at the White House. As president, Roosevelt appointed Bat U.S. deputy marshal in New York, and Bat reciprocated with introductions to sports figures he knew the President admired. In the Oval Office of the White House, Roosevelt listened, enchanted, to the stories Bat told of the Wild West. There was the thrilling Battle of Adobe Walls, tall tales of the Earps at the OK Corral, and of Dodge City when the herds came in and wild Texans tried to take over the town.

His journalist friend, William Lewis, was now editor of the *New York Morning Telegraph*, and gave Bat a job writing a sports column. The somewhat raffish paper was definitely Bat's style, with an informal city room where copy-readers played poker between writing head-lines, and chorus girls sat on desks waiting for their reporter boyfriends.

President Roosevelt offered Bat the post of U.S. Marshal of Oklahoma Territory. Bat refused, pointing out to the president he had hung up his guns for good and had no desire to be forced to kill some drunken young fool who wanted a reputation as the gunfighter who killed Bat Masterson.

In 1921 Bat was 67 years old, mellow and good-natured. On October 25, shortly before noon, Bat strolled up Eighth Avenue from his apartment to the newspaper office and wrote his column for the next day. Fifteen minutes after he finished it, he died alone in his office, slumped over his rolltop desk. When found, his last column was clutched in his hand.

Bat's death was reported on the front page of the afternoon editions, one of which said, "He died at his desk gripping his pen with the tenacity with which he formerly clung to his six-shooter."

Bat Masterson had always predicted he would die with his boots on. And that's what he did.

Famous
Gun Fighters of the
Western Frontier

Fifth Article. "Billy" Tilghman

By W. B. (Bat) MASTERSON

One of the most durable and lovable of Western marshals portrayed on television was Bat Masterson. Gene Barry actually looked like Bat, with the same natty style.

Wyatt Earp
Brave, Courageous and Bold

Long may he live, in fame and glory
And long may his story be told.
    . . . Theme song of an Earp TV series

*

The big guy, rail-thin but strong, stood under the canvas shading Brennan's Saloon in the Kansas cattle town of Ellsworth. He wore no guns. A white linen shirt set off his bronzed features, his broadcloth trousers were tucked into short boots. He was 25 years old, and his name was Wyatt Earp.

He was not then famous—but he would be.

Ellsworth was a rollicking, riotous trail-end town, and a couple of hell-raisers had just fired a fatal load of buckshot into the sheriff on this sweltering August day. "It's none of my business," said Earp to the mayor, "but if it was me I'd get me a gun and arrest the guy or kill him." The mayor quickly hung a badge on Earp's shirt. "I'll make it your business," he told the lanky stranger. "Here's your badge. Get some guns. I order you to arrest that killer."

And what that career was, seems to be the subject of much controversy. In his own autobiography, as told to writer Stuart Lake, he was the hero of every encounter. The facts don't always bear that out.

But this much appears clear. First, he didn't linger long in Ellsworth, but moved on to the Wichita, where he found that the fame of his Ellsworth event had preceded him. "You the fellow that run it over Ben Thompson?" the mayor asked. Earp scarcely had time to answer before the deputy marshal's star was pinned to his chest.

It didn't take long before Wichita proved too tame, so Earp moved on, this time to Dodge City—called "Queen of the Cowtowns" . . . "Wickedest Little City in America" . . . "Gomorrah of the Plains" . . . all rolled into one throbbing package. It was a paradise for gamblers, girls and gunmen. Early newsprint described it as "the place where a man can break all Ten Commandments in one night."

The responsibility for taming all this exuberance went to Wyatt Earp and his three lieutenants—Bat and Jim Masterson and Joe Mason. For keeping law and order, he was paid $250 a month, plus a bonus of $2.50 for each arrest. He kept the jail full.

There's little doubt, however, that he was able to supplement that meager stipend from other sources. At the town's leading saloon, the Long Branch, he more than doubled his peace-officer's pay by moonlighting as a dealer of faro and monte, the card games most popular with frontier gamblers. As a dealer, Wyatt took a percentage of the house winnings; as an officer of the law, he saw to it that sullen losers made orderly departures from the premises.

Wyatt Earp is seated second in front row, Bat Masterson stands far right, back row.

Those were lively days in Dodge, when it was a thoroughfare as celebrated in world news as, say, Fifth Avenue. A sign at the corner of Bridge Street announced that the carrying of firearms within the city limits was forbidden by any but peace officers, and Wyatt Earp saw to it that no one argued about it. One night in the Long Branch Saloon, backed by Bat Masterson, he called the bluff of Clay Allison, one of the West's most notable psychopathic killers, branded him a coward and drove him out of town.

But as the months went by, life in Dodge City lost its savor. The cattle herds that had made the town lively, now passed Dodge by. Bat Masterson was no longer sheriff. Earp had turned in his star. Dodge was settling down into a slumbering prairie community. The Wild West was running out of steam.

A new jolt of excitement developed, though, with news of a booming silver strike in Arizona, which meant there might be more money lying around loose in Tombstone. So Earp packed up his guns and headed for Tombstone. There he was joined by his brothers Virgil, Morgan and Jim. Doc Holliday and his common-law wife, Big Nose Kate, soon followed, and later Bat Masterson.

Tombstone, like Dodge in its early days, was a violent town. Few days passed without a shooting or a killing. At the time Earp was appointed deputy sheriff, southeastern Arizona was terrorized by bands of rustlers, horse thieves, and desperadoes, loosely classified as "the cowboy element." Chief among the plundering bands was the Clanton clan, a large ranching family of hard-drinking riders led by "Old Man" Clanton. His son Ike was to figure dramatically in the future of Wyatt Earp.

Earp's troubles began on the night of March 15, 1881, when a stage coach left Tombstone carrying eight passengers and a load of bullion. Along the line, bandits tried to halt the coach, and in so doing killed the driver and one passenger. Doc Holliday was arrested on reasonable suspicion (the charge lacked evidence) and the Earps were rumored to be the brains behind the bungled holdup. The arrest was made by sheriff Behan, who maintained a friendship with the cowboy-rustler faction, whose votes he coveted. There was no love lost between Behan and the Earps. The stage was now set for one of the most famous gunfights of the West—at the OK Corral.

The long countdown to the climax of the quarrel has endless facets and must be omitted for space reasons. Suffice it to say, vicious hatred now raged between the rival factions.

News reached the Earps that their enemies were at the OK Corral—two Clantons and three other miscreants. Wyatt and Morgan set out, were joined by Holliday. Then Virgil appeared. They walked in line abreast, dressed in black hats and long black frock coats, as was their custom. When Behan spotted them he asked Virgil, who was a marshal, to disarm "the boys," not fight. But he was brushed aside by Virgil, who outranked a sheriff. Wyatt and Morgan had already been deputized, now Virgil turned to Holliday and deputized him, handing him a shotgun.

Before they even reached the OK Corral, the rustler gang appeared. If the cowboys felt trapped, they did not show it. Though ill-prepared, the cowboys now took the initiative. In the silence, a click, click could be heard as two men cocked their holstered six-shooters. "Hold! I want your guns," Virgil Earp called out. Then someone shouted, "Son-of-a-bitch"— and the next words were lost in the first exchange of shots. Eyewitnesses later testified to the swirling, deadly melee.

It took less than a minute before it was all over. Three of the rustlers lay dead. Morgan Earp was hit in the left shoulder, Virgil in the leg, Holliday in the hip. Only Ike Clanton and Wyatt Earp escaped injury. Suddenly the shooting stopped; gun smoke drifted over a silent scene.

As depicted by staff artists of The Illustrated Police, the OK battle has little relation to factual reality. The Earps wore the traditional slouch hats, single-breasted black frock coats and flowing black ties. None had long hair, and all were clean shaven except for handlebar mustaches.

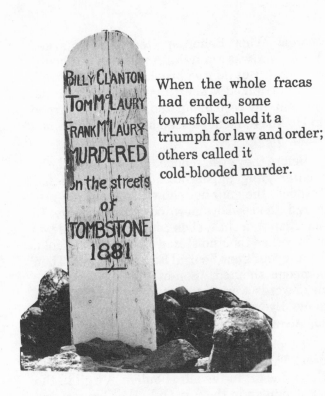

When the whole fracas had ended, some townsfolk called it a triumph for law and order; others called it cold-blooded murder.

In any case, friends of those slain took matters into their own hands. One day Virgil Earp was ambushed and wounded, shattering his left arm. "Don't worry," he told his wife, "I've still got one arm to hug you." Morgan Earp was picked off in the middle of a billiards game by a sharpshooter who fired through a window from a back alley, killing him.

Wyatt Earp, now deputized by a federal marshall, rode off with several other gunmen in pursuit of his brother's killer. He rode and he rode, but he never came back.

In the years that followed, he graced a number of western towns with his presence, dealing faro, moving on. Sometimes he ran into Bat Masterson. As late as 1911 he was accused of complicity in a confidence game. But in the main he was straight, living his later days in San Diego, California.

While in San Diego, Earp acquired the first of the thoroughbred racehorses which were to command his attention for the ensuing decade. In fact, he added considerably to his means in San Diego, purchasing property with an apparent unlimited supply of money.

He used some of the property to open three gambling halls. Each of them featured 21 different games of faro, blackjack, poker and keno. To the delight of all, Earp was known to make the rounds of his casinos, dealing faro as in the old days.

A veteran gambler who knew Earp in both Tombstone and San Diego wrote, "A man could lose his money as easily in San Diego as in Tombstone, but the odds on saving his life were better in the halls of San Diego."

Gradually Earp sold most of his San Diego investments, but he continued to pop in frequently to play cards at the Silver Strand, near Coronado, where a popular tent city catered to vacationers. Whenever things got out of hand with an occasional "rough and tumble" gambler, Earp would personally see to it that order was restored with his still agile fists.

Wyatt Earp lived to the ripe old age of 80—a rare feat for a gunfighter.

As portrayed by Hugh O'Brien on television, and in various paperbacks and coloring books, Wyatt Earp had lost his magnificent handlebar mustache and was now wearing a patterned vest.

Among his other claims to fame, Wyatt Earp once played a leading role in one of the most controversial fights in America's ring history.

It was 1896 and the big event was the Sharkey-Fitzsimmons heavyweight fight in San Francisco. When neither of the fight managers could agree on a referee, Wyatt Earp was chosen. Even then, Fitzsimmon's manager charged that Earp had been "fixed" and delayed the fight before an impatient, jeering crowd.

Earp was finally summoned from a nearby restaurant. Then the fight was further delayed when a police captain told Earp he'd have to relieve himself of the gun he was wearing.

That detail disposed of, the fight began, and for seven rounds Fitzsimmons pounded Sharkey. But during the eighth, Sharkey suddenly clutched his groin and, writhing with pain, fell to the canvas. While the bewildered audience looked on, Earp gave the bout to Sharkey because of Fitzsimmon's "foul blow."

That fight is still debated by ring historians.

ADVERTISING GAIN,
2155 More Ads
During November, 1896.
—
During November, 1896.

The Examiner.

CIRCULATION GAIN,
903 Copies Daily
NET PAID AVERAGE CIRCULATION,
OCTOBER increase over
SEPTEMBER, 1896.

VOL. LXIII.   SAN FRANCISCO: THURSDAY MORNING, DECEMBER 3, 1896.   NO. 155.

"SHARKEY WINS BY A FOUL," SAID REFEREE EARP.

Although Declared the Victor He Was Writhing on the Floor When the Decision Was Given in His Favor.

FITZSIMMONS ACCUSES EARP OF FRAUD.

I was simply robbed out of $10,000 by that decision, and what is more, I knew I was going to be robbed before I entered the ring.

...I made that speech to the crowd telling them that Earp as referee notwithstanding the information ...brought to me that he had been fixed to throw ..., I knew that I was a goner. But what ... had refused to fight the whole country ... as afraid to meet the man who

... of the world was at stake
three times $10,000. The
...Sharkey and I could not
...the selection of one.
... to agree to any
...rong, but I
until he

SHARKEY DESCRIBES THAT DECISIVE BLOW.

With the exception of an awful pain in my groin I cannot say that I feel any the worse for my encounter with Fitzsimmons. I did my very best during the contest ... to sleep and am satisfied that I had the best round.

Fitzsimmons pretends to be a ...
a knack of making himself appe...
But the truth of it is he use...
ever met
His principal ...
his elbow on
deep gash
durin

WYATT EARP, WHOSE DECISION MEANT $10,000.

Doc Holliday

The Deadly Dentist

It would be impossible to recount the riveting saga of the Earps in the wild, lawless West without running into the ghost of Wyatt's consumptive, homicidal dentist friend, the notorious "Doc" Holliday.

John H. Holliday, DDS

DENTISTRY.
J. H. Holliday, Dentist, very respectfully offers his professional services to the citizens of Dodge City and surrounding country during the summer. Office at room No. 24, Dodge House. Where satisfaction is not given money will be refunded.

His shingle

Georgia-born, Holliday's family, though impoverished, somehow scraped together enough money to send him to college. He fled Georgia after killing two black men who insisted on sharing a swimming pool near his home.

He next appeared in Dallas, where he put out his shingle, "J.H. Holliday, Dentist." But he liked poker better than dentistry and usually patients had to seek him out in he gaming rooms. When a rancher accused him of cheating, Doc killed him.

Forced once again to flee, he landed near a military reservation, and soon was on the run for killing a soldier. With a posse on his heels, he rode 800 miles alone through the Texas Panhandle to Denver, where he hid out. But there, within a few weeks, he carved up a young man who somehow lived to tell about it. Following the stabbing, Holliday rode into Dodge, where he met Wyatt Earp. According to Bat Masterson, "Doc idolized him."

Dentist by trade and gambler by choice, he arrived in Dodge City about the same time as the Earps, to set up his dentist's office on the second floor of Dodge House. Thereafter he gambled his way through almost every boom camp in the West. When the Earps moved on to Tombstone, Arizona Territory, Doc and his big-nosed mistress, Kate Elder, soon followed.

He was Wyatt Earp's devoted friend. He is said to have saved Wyatt's life from a mob of drunken cowboys on one occasion, and stood by his friend at the famous gunfight at the OK Corral.

In fact, Wyatt Earp may have been his only friend. There was little to like about Doc Holliday. In a contemporary account, Bat Masterson said he "had a mean disposition and an ungovernable temper, was hot-headed and impetuous and much given to both drinking and quarreling. He was very much disliked, and under the influence of liquor was a most dangerous man."

He was a familiar figure in the roaring days of Tombstone, a tiny man emaciated with tuberculosis, who constantly coughed blood into his handkerchief. He carried a nickel-plated six-shooter, a bowie knife tied around his neck by a string, and sometimes a sawed-off shotgun stuck in his belt. He had pale blue eyes, a wispy, sandy mustache, and blond hair.

His sweetheart, Big Nose Kate, once burned down a hotel in Texas to rescue him after he had been held for a killing.

After the gunfight at OK Corral, the Earps went to Gunnison, and Doc left for Pueblo, Colorado, where he became a fixture in the gaming room of the Comique Club. Most of the gamblers, bartenders and the police knew about his part in the OK Corral "street fight," and Doc became something of celebrity.

There was a brief skirmish with the law when his past caught up with him, and a bounty hunter of sorts tracked hm down and accused him of the murders of Clanton and others in Dodge. Doc got in touch with Bat Masterson, then in Trinidad, who came and made a few skillful moves that got Doc off the hook and out of jail.

There was one last act of violence. Doc shot a Leadville bartender over a $5 loan. Doc knew he was slipping when it took two shots to give the man a flesh wound in the arm. He was acquitted, but at the end of the trial he was escorted to a stage leaving for Colorado Springs. He was no longer welcome in Leadville.

By the next spring, he was very frail, his body shaken by constant coughing spells. Someone told him that the hot springs at Glenwood Springs were beneficial for tuberculosis. But within two weeks he became bedridden. He died in 1885 at the age of 35. On his deathbed he asked for a last drink of whiskey, then raised his head, looked down at his feet, and whispered, "Well, I'll be damned."

Doc had always sworn he would die with his boots on. They were off.

Kate Fisher, better known as Big Nose Kate.

The words on his tombstone read:

DOC HOLLIDAY 1852–1887
HE DIED IN BED

Wild Bill Hickok
Prince of the Pistoleers

A century after his death, "Wild Bill" Hickok remains perhaps the most famous gunfighter of them all, his legend greatly enhanced by his own gross exaggeration of his accomplishments, and by the published stories of awestruck journalists who believed his imaginative accounts.

Once interviewed by H. M. Stanley (later to achieve fame for tracking down Dr. Livingstone), Hickok bragged, "I would be willing to take an oath on the Bible that I have killed over a hundred men."

Inquired Stanley, "Did you kill them without cause or provocation?" Replied Hickok, "No, by heaven, I never killed one man without good cause."

More painstaking research has reduced the number of substantiated slayings to seven.

Although he was indeed a crack shot, he concocted fabulous lies, always making himself out to be a hero. One of his feats, he claimed, was picking off 50 Confederates with 50 bullets and a wonder-working rifle.

Still there is plenty of evidence that the man was actually a hero at times. As an Army scout, he rescued 34 men from an Indian siege by galloping through the attackers to seek help.

In his years before becoming Abilene's marshal, he was a constable, a stagecoach driver, a wagonmaster in the Civil War, scout, courier and spy.

He spent eight months as Abilene's marshal, most of it in the spacious Alamo Saloon. His reputation with a gun was such that he was in perpetual fear of assassination by glory hunters; he left street-patrolling to others.

He picked the wrong greenie to trim.

His Gun

.45-calibre Deane-Adams English 5-shot

In October, after most of the cowboys had gone back to Texas, Wild Bill had one of his most controversial gunfights. Reports are conflicting, but the trouble appears to have started when a gambler named Coe headed for a showdown with Hickok, surrounded by about 50 Texans. When the melee ended, Coe was severely wounded, Hickok was grazed by bullets, and Hickok's best friend, who had run into the line of fire, was killed.

The city council fired Hickok; after that his career was all downhill. He wandered from place to place, for a brief period was an actor in Buffalo Bill's Wild West Show. Cody had to sack him when he found out Hickok got stage fright and couldn't utter a line.

The end came in Deadwood, Dakota Territory. He was making an indifferent living from gambling. He was going blind from glaucoma. One afternoon a whiskey-soaked hired assassin named Jack McCall sneaked up behind him as he was playing cards at Carl Mann's Saloon, with his back to the door, and shot him in the head. Hickok fell face forward across the table.

———

Later, somebody thought to look at the cards he held. They were aces and eights, a hand known from then on throughout the West as the "deadman's hand."

THOMAS J. SMITH

MARSHAL OF ABILENE, 1870

DIED A MARTYR TO DUTY NOV. 2, 1870

A FEARLESS HERO OF FRONTIER DAYS

WHO IN COWBOY CHAOS

ESTABLISHED THE SUPREMACY OF THE LAW.

When Hickok came to Abilene as marshal, he replaced Tom Smith, a two-fisted fighter who didn't like guns. A disgruntled cowboy shot him in the back.

In the movie version, as played by Guy Madison, Wild Bill had gone for a shave and haircut.

Teddy Roosevelt
A Deputy Sheriff

Teddy Roosevelt: rancher and Billings County deputy sheriff

Strangest of western law enforcers was the man who would become the 26th president of the United States.

Theodore Roosevelt was twenty-four years old when he first came to Dakota Territory on a vacation to shoot buffalo. His arrival on the dying frontier was barely a decade after Custer's fateful rout, yet buffalo were already almost extinct. So the hunting party had to ride far into the Badlands in their search for game.

During the course of that journey, Teddy Roosevelt fell in love with the beautiful savage country and made up his mind to become part of it.

He was also impressed by stories of quick riches to be made from cattle ranching. The vast grasslands that had sustained buffalo herds and Indians for centuries were now owned by the railroads, which got it all for nothing and were glad to sell it cheap. So before Teddy boarded the Northern Pacific to return to the political life of the East, he bought some acreage and a thousand head of cattle, and made arrangements to have a ranch house built.

Back home in the East, he was hit by a double tragedy: his wife died in childbirth, and his mother died of typhoid fever. It was a tough blow, and the only cure he could find to ease the pain was to return to the harsh outdoor life of the Dakota prairies.

So in spring he returned to Medora, settled into his new ranch house with his books and horse, riding as many as 70 miles a day. His singular toughness quickly made him part of the rough rancher role.

One of his first acts in his new life was to have a local seamstress make him a buckskin shirt, which he said was "the most distinctively national dress in America." Later he added a broad sombrero, horsehide chaps, cowboy boots and silver spurs to his costume.

He made a rather odd appearing cowboy. His pale face with its short reddish mustache over a mouthful of big teeth and his large round eyeglasses reminded his compatriots of an owl. One day, as he entered the bar of some small cattletown hotel, he heard gunshots. Inside, a drunken bully was swaggering, firing off his pistol into the air. When he saw Teddy he roared, "Four-Eyes is going to treat!"

Teddy ignored the rowdy for a while, but when he started to use foul language, a gun in each hand, the "tenderfoot" rose. "He was foolish to stand so near me," he later wrote in his memoirs, "and his heels were so close together he could be easily toppled." Teddy had been a boxing champ at Harvard. "I struck quick and hard with my right as I rose, hitting with my left as I straightened out, then again with my right. He fired the gun but I do not know whether it was a convulsive action of his hand or if he was trying to shoot me. When he went down he struck the corner of the bar with his head." The bartender hauled the unconscious gunman off to a shed and locked him in. The next day the hoodlum left town on freight.

After this incident, Teddy lost his tenderfoot image. He was loved and respected by the cowboys, who made him chairman of the Stockmen's Association. As such he also became a deputy sheriff, bound (at least by his own moral code) to carry out the law.

It was during the spring of 1886 that Roosevelt experienced a splendid Western adventure, which began with the theft of a boat he kept moored on the river bank. Evidence pointed to a rangy, hard-eyed badman named "Redhead" Finnegan and his followers, a German of dubious mentality and a half-breed Indian.

Roosevelt was outraged, and in spite of a raging blizzard and the fact his foreman had to build a scow to pursue the thieves, he was off on a manhunt. He later wrote an account of his adventure, "Sheriff's Work on a Ranch." Excerpts reflect all the excitement of a real Wild West capture.

"There could have been no better men than my two companions - tough, hardy, resolute fellows, quick as cats, strong as bears, and able to travel like bull moose. The weather had been bitterly cold, as a furious blizzard was blowing, but the day we left there was a lull. We dressed warmly with wool socks, heavy trousers and great fur coats.

"The river twisted in every direction, and we drifted swiftly between heaped-up piles of ice, sometimes eight or ten feet high. During the night the temperature went down to zero

"We were always on the alert, keeping a sharp lookout. Finally our watchfulness was rewarded. On the third day we saw the lost boat moored against the bank, and smoke was curling up from a campfire.

"The only one in camp was the German, whose weapons were on the ground. The other two were off hunting. He surrendered instantly, and we sat down to wait for the others. We heard them a long way off and made ready. I shouted to them to hold up their hands — an order that in the West a man is bound not to disregard. The half-breed obeyed at once, his knees buckling with terror. Finnegan hesitated, his eyes fairly wolfish; then as I walked a few paces, covering his chest, he saw he had no show and, with an oath, let his rifle drop and held his hands beside his head.

The capture of Finnegan

47

"The next eight days were as irksome and monotonous as any I ever spent. There is little amusement in combining the functions of a sheriff with those of an arctic explorer."

Ice jams blocked the river; they were in country of unfriendly Sioux Indians; the stock of provisions grew scanty; they had to be on constant guard over their prisoners. "So long as we kept watchful, the prisoners understood any attempt at a break would result in being shot. But it was harassing, tedious work, and the strain, day in day out without let-up, became tiresome."

At last they landed in the cow camp of a ranch. Teddy managed to hire a wagon and some mares, with a driver (who wondered why he was going to so much trouble over a couple of thieves), to take his prisoners to turn them in.

"My three captives were unarmed, but I was alone with them except for the driver, and I soon found the safest plan was to put them in the wagon and myself walk behind with the inevitable Winchester. The mares could only drag the wagon at a walk, so it took two days and a night to make the journey. At night we put up at a squalid granger's hut, the only habitation on our road. I did not dare to go to sleep, and spent the night sitting with my back against the cabin door.

"I was most heartily glad when we at last jolted into the long, straggling main street of Dickinson, and I was able to give my unwilling companions into the hands of the sheriff.

"Under the laws of Dakota I received my fees as a deputy sheriff for making the three arrests, and also mileage for the three hundred odd miles gone over — a total of some fifty dollars."

Theodore Roosevelt as he liked to think of himself.

Order in the Court

That first year of the California gold rush, there was surprisingly little crime. Nuggets were so plentiful it was simpler to go out and find gold than to steal it. Problems were dealt with on the basis of "letting the punishment fit the crime." One miscreant who stole a sack of gold hastily repented after he was tied to a tree near a creek, his back laid bare to the bloodthirsty mosquitos.

Judge Brown holds court in Tuttletown, Calif.

Later, when the smell of money brought thieves and cutthroats to the diggings, lynching became a solution. Mining camps had no courts or judges; "justice" was swift and final.

More serious were the problems that developed in San Francisco, gateway to the gold fields. A village of no more than 500 souls, it was suddenly swollen by thousands of goldseekers and a loose element it wasn't prepared to cope with.

When John Geary became mayor in 1849, he made it clear how desperate the situation was: "You are without a single police officer or judge, and have not the means of confining a prisoner for an hour."

The situation made a fertile breeding ground for flagrant crime. Chief among the rowdy element were the Hounds, whose mission it was to rid the city of foreigners, and the Sydney Ducks, former members of Britain's prison colony in Australia.

One night the Hounds raided a Chilean village, savaged a young girl, stole what they wanted and burned down the rest. San Francisco was shocked out of its apathy and formed a volunteer police force of 230 businessmen who were also judge and jury. Within hours the Hounds were rounded up, a trial was held, and nine were convicted. There was no jail, so the sentence pronounced was exile with the threat of lynching should they return.

During the year the Vigilantes were active, leading underworld members were tracked down and banished (three were lynched). Crime dropped sharply, in spite of the lack of formal jurisprudence.

Seal of the San Francisco Vigilance Committee "We Never Sleep"

But even after California was populated, there was a vast wilderness between West and East. Today's Americans are not particularly impressed by the immensity of the United States, but a century or more ago, the West was rugged, often desolate land, to be conquered only by those strong enough to tame it.

Often a saloon keeper was the judge. In Gold Hill, Nevada the bartender also recorded mining claims in a book behind the bar. In after-years, millions of dollars hinged on these scribbled notes.

Law and order were slow to follow, and people were obliged to make their own laws and dispense justice on the spot.

Early courtroom justice was makeshift at best. Judges with formal education hadn't yet made their way into the Wild West, so some responsible storekeeper might serve, using his shop as the courtroom.

Eventually, however, continuing violence forced communities to build facilities and pay a qualified judge.

He didn't always get the respect his position deserved. Some citizens resented any rein on their freedom and liked the old system better. Many a judge was cursed out to his face, subjected by spectators to a display of pistols and bowie knives. The irreverence of Dodge City residents moved one judge to announce, "Any person caught throwing turnips, cigar stumps, or old quids of tobacco at this court will be immediately arraigned before this bar of justice."

The problems of the bench were many. Lawyers were abysmally ignorant of the law; only a few had been formally schooled. Judges had to advise both the prosecution and the defense on rules of procedure. Geography alone made his task a formidable one. Often he had to take long, toilsome, circuit-riding trips to try accused malefactors being detained in various communities within his sprawling jurisdiction. Rounding up enough citizens to form a jury was difficult in thinly settled areas, and not all of them were too bright. Mark Twain recalled one Virginia City juror who thought that "incest and arson were the same thing."

But for all the failings of the district court, it was there that the Western criminal first met the cutting edge of lawbook law.

And in time the more thoughtful elements in the community came to see that courts were an essential aid to local peacekeeping efforts. It was all well and good for a marshal to hunt down an evildoer at high risk, but unless the man was tried and punished, the risk was likely to recur.

Few of the judges who sentenced the West's criminals are remembered today except by specialists, but two remain frontier immortals—Judge Roy Bean and the "hanging judge," Isaac Parker.

50

Honorable Isaac Parker
The Hanging Judge

He built a gallows that would hang twelve felons at a time. Yet he was a gentle man, a devout Christian, and he cleaned up an outlaws' hangout as no other lawyer or judge could.

At the time, there was no worse judicial mess in the nation than in Indian Territory–that vast wilderness area wedged between Arkansas and Texas which eventually turned into the state of Oklahoma.

The 50,000 Indians who lived there were, by treaty, self-governing and responsible for their own law and order. But they had no authority whatsoever over any white population that wandered in.

It was a rogue's paradise!

Every fleeing miscreant could find safe haven in Indian Territory, a situation well delineated in the motion picture "True Grit."

The U.S. court designated to deal with this lawless empire was the District Court at Fort Smith, Arkansas, a mere hundred yards off the eastern edge, where one single judge was expected to administer justice over 70,000 square miles infested with outlaws.

For Judge William Story, this was no problem. He simply did nothing. Terrorized travelers came and went; cries of alarm and indignation arose from the Indians. In one year 100 murders conveniently escaped his notice.

Then, as if in answer to the prayers of both Washington and the Indians, a brilliant man actually volunteered for the job. He was Isaac Parker–lawyer, ex-judge and ex-Congressman–who asked for the assignment because he wanted to help the Indians.

Parker was a fine figure of a man, handsome, six feet tall, a devout Methodist with a stern look about him that spoke of Authority.

He arrived at Fort Smith with his wife and children, and as Mrs. Parker looked around the town that was to be her new home, she said, "Isaac, we have made a great mistake." Her husband replied, "No, Mary, we are faced with a great task. These people need us."

Eight days later, Parker eased himself into the high-backed chair of his court, to face a backlog of 91 cases to be tried. He went through them with determination and dispatch.

The cases were typical of the West. One man had murdered a cowboy to get his fancy boots and saddle. Another had knifed an old friend for his pocket money. Another had borrowed a friend's rifle, then on a whim used it to kill his friend. Judge Parker tried all 91 cases in eight weeks of his first session, eighteen being charged with murder, with fifteen convicted. Of the fifteen, six were condemned to death.

Sentencing them, Parker told them, "I do not desire to hang you men. It is the law." Then, unaccountably, his eyes filled with tears.

But hang them he did. Six at a time. Five thousand people came to see the spectacle in the compound of the fort. There were children present, the clergy had come, and some hymn singing was heard.

A special gallows had been built, capable of hanging a dozen men at a time. George Maledon was in charge, making sure that the six dropped simultaneously to a swift death. "I never hanged a man who came back to have the job done over," he later recalled with gallows humor.

The event was played up by newsmen, especially in the East, where many readers were horrified. There arose a hue and a cry that public hanging was inhuman–a charge that was to grow in volume in succeeding years.

But Parker was busy with other matters. Besides his duties as a judge, he wanted to organize a system for bringing in more of the lawbreakers who were hiding out in Indian Territory, bring them to trial.

In flushing out the lawbreakers, Parker had to face reality. He didn't like gunfighters, but he knew it took one to catch one. He made an attempt to screen out the outright crooks. But if he thought the man could do the job, he overlooked possible blotches in the man's past. In any case, deputies weren't anxious to shoot to kill, because every prisoner they could bring to trial meant an arrest fee of two dollars, whereas a corpse brought nothing. They got 10¢ a mile one way for serving papers or bringing in a prisoner, plus 40¢ a mile to feed him.

There was very little job security in being a deputy. In Parker's two decades of tenure, 65 of his deputies, out of 225, died on the job.

With all this rushing in and flushing out, Parker's case load became horrendous. Over the years in office, juries brought in 8,600 guilty verdicts and 1,700 acquittals. Often it was hard to scrape up a jury, and jurors who came from a distance weren't anxious to hang around waiting for the trial to begin. So Judge Parker pushed his cases through in record time. In one case, where a group of five men were accused of both rape and murder, he ran the rape case through, then switched juries and ran the murder case through. He got double convictions on the accused men, but of course they had to hang only once each.

There was no coddling in the Fort Smith court. The Judge's piercing blue eyes often glared down on evil-doers from 8 a.m. until far into the night, after which he'd walk the mile to his home in the dark, never wearing a gun.

By 1889 it was obvious to everyone, except possibly Judge Parker, that the case load was simply too heavy for one man. Congress made the first of several moves to cut down his territory. Parker protested mildly. Then Congress made a more direct attack on the Hanging Judge, empowering the Supreme Court to hear appeals from prisoners at Fort Smith. Much of the time, Parker's decisions were reversed.

Parker's old-style methods of rule, so vital in the early years of outlaw violence, were outdated. As he said himself, "During the twenty years I have administered the law here, the contest has been one between civilization and savagery." But Judge Parker was a fading frontier figure, incapable of adjusting to change.

In the end, his territory was cut to pitiful size, and the Indians he had tried to protect were rousted out of their territory by the invasion of white citizens who wanted to build on their land.

He died in 1896 from diabetes, which no one knew he had, and at last the worth of the man was proclaimed. But the tributes that would have touched him most came from the Indians who knew his worth as few whites did. One of them, a Creek chief, brought wild flowers to his funeral.

John Wayne played a Judge Parker deputy in "True Grit." Portrayal of Indian Territory and the carnival aura of the hanging was surprisingly true to life.

Judge Roy Bean
Judge, Jury and Bartender

His Honor

Kentucky-born Roy Bean had a lively life, some of it illegal, before departing from his wife and children in an area of San Antonio that later came to be known as Beanville. His adventures stretched from Mexico to San Diego before he decided that his future lay in following the Southern Pacific Railroad as it was extended westward, to serve whiskey to thirsty construction crews.

By now pressing sixty, gray, portly and whiskey-sodden, Roy Bean at last settled in a town called Langtry, which he claimed he named after his idol, but which Southern Pacific said was named after one of its own dignitaries.

Bean set himself up in business there with a copy of the Revised Statutes of Texas, a smattering of legal jargon and a strong personality, in a 14' x 20' shack complete with bar, poker tables, jury box, and bench. He was, he proudly proclaimed, "the law west of the Pecos." And so he was, for the nearest court was some 200 miles away.

The Judge is in.

Judge Roy Bean was a soiled and whiskered corpulent man who had three passions. One was the law (he loved to fine people). Another was whiskey (in adult portions). The third was Lily Langtry, famed actress and one-time vivacious mistress to Britain's Prince of Wales. He named his saloon after her—the Jersey Lilly (her sobriquet), misspelled by a painter who had sampled too long at the bar.

The saloon was also the Judge's courtroom.

In our time, he seems amusing. And he certainly gave plenty of laughs in his own day. But the victims, especially when he was in what might politely be called a capricious mood, can scarcely have seen the joke.

Bean's verdicts were liable to make legal history—of a sort. On one occasion he turned himself into a coroner as well as the judge. A railroad worker, who had fallen several hundred feet from a viaduct, was pronounced dead by Bean, who then decided that the five-dollar coroner's fee was insufficient. So he switched himself from coroner to justice of the peace, examined the body and found a pistol and $40. "I find this corpse," he boomed gravely, "guilty of carrying a concealed weapon, I fine it $40!"

Perhaps his most famous—infamous by today's standards—ruling was in favor of a railroad hand who was a good customer at the liquor end of the bar. When the Irishman got hauled in for killing a Chinese laborer, bringing a hundred other Irish roustabouts with him, the Judge leafed through his law book and solemnly ruled that "there ain't a damn line here that makes it illegal to kill a Chinaman. The defendant is discharged."

On another occasion, when another kindred soul was charged with blowing daylight into a Mexican, the Judge ruled that "it served the deceased right for getting in front of a gun."

He ruled over Langtry for twenty years, first by appointment, then by election (held in his saloon), settling cases mostly by common sense.

The Judge had a variety of profitable lines. He got $5 a head for officiating at inquests, and $2 to $5 for presiding at weddings and divorces. His marriage ceremonies always ended with a pronouncement used by more orthodox jurists in levying death sentences: "May God have mercy on your soul."

Bean did get one look at the lady he had so much admired from her picture in a magazine. Lily Langtry played San Antonio on her American tour in the spring of 1888. Bean got himself dressed up in fancy duds, went to the theater and got a front-row seat. That's as close as he ever got.

The actress did make a trip to Langtry five years later, after hearing he had named his saloon after her. But Roy Bean had died eight months earlier. The townsfolk were entranced and gave her the Judge's pet bear which he had kept chained to his bedpost for years. When the bear ran away, not knowing the lady, they gave Lily the Judge's revolver.

She said she would hang it in a place of honor in her home, a reminder of a funny old secret admirer she never knew at all.

The Mavericks

If the westering movement attracted the violent and the unruly, it also attracted a legion of nonconformists. Mavericks, eccentrics, adventurers, they were men of independent mind and rugged individuality who marched to a different drummer, and found in the West the perfect setting to live as they pleased.

Some were daring, some courageous, some flamboyant; they all helped shape the colorful fabric of the early, wild West.

Take Grizzly Adams, for one. He fled the humdrum life of a New England cobbler in 1849 to take up a hermit's existence in California. "I was dead broke, I was disgusted with my fellow men and their hypocrisy."

In the eight years he spent in the Sierra mountains, he had enough adventure to hold a man for a century.

He became a tamer of wild animals, including the dreaded California grizzly, the most dangerous animal on the continent. In doing so, he collected considerable scar tissue. But he also made friends with them, used them to carry his packs and, from time to time, even rode on their backs.

His possessions were a bedroll, two fine hunting rifles, a battered wagon and two oxen that were so feeble he claimed he had to lift them by the tail to get them to stand on their feet. In time, though, he opened a Mountaineer Museum in San Francisco, where his menagerie of bears, wolves, mountain lions, elk, deer and other wild animals soon brought him fame. He went on the stage locally, and in 1860 sailed for New York where he entered a partnership with Phineas T. Barnum.

An adventurer of a different sort was Frederic Remington, who fell in love with the West and lived for a season or two with cowboys and with Indians, in order to portray their "hard as nails" life in sketches and sculpture. No tenderfoot, he quickly became as expert as an old cowhand in a western saddle.

One of the most persistent of rugged western individualists was the circuit-riding preacher. It was said that whenever a new territory was opened up, the first to arrive were the whiskey seller and the missionary. Often his pulpit was in the saloon, for a church was definitely not one of the first structures in a new settlement.

The God of the American West, it was said, did his good work from the saddle. The Methodist bishop Asbury traveled 270,000 miles in ministering to his western flock. Father de Smet covered more than 180,000 miles. Their efforts were ill paid. One itinerant parson in Indiana received nine dollars and a pair of new pants for a year's work.

Many preachers were indistinguishable from the gamblers—a long black coat, white shirt, and string tie were the trademark of both. One wandering preacher was described as long-legged, cadaverous and melancholy, wearing a black wide-brimmed and low-crowned hat. He sported s scraggly beard of the variety known as Galway choker and carried a large Bible under one arm, waving a horsewhip with the other. He had a bowie knife stuck in one boot and an old rimfire revolver in the other, "which discouraged over-familiarity."

Preaching was muscular and flavorful, otherwise it made no impact. One Reverend exhorted players in a gambling saloon to repent, so that when death overtook them they could "call *keno!* and rake in the heavenly pot."

Calamity Jane, who spent a great deal of time inside saloons, once passed the hat for an itinerant preacher outside a saloon in Deadwood. She exhorted the crowd, "You sinners, dig down in your pockets now, this old fellow looks as though he was broke and I want to collect about two hundred dollars for him!" She easily made the sum.

Reverend John Dyer, an early Methodist circuit rider, often preached in saloons.

Whatever role these free spirits played in the epic drama of the taming of the West, they were tough of fiber and filled with the vigorous juice of life.

They were nonconformists in a time and a place that will not be seen again.

Prince of the highway was the man who drove the stagecoach. He was honored by waystation keepers, revered by his passengers (whose lives were in his hands), and turned into legend by news reporters.

Driving a stagecoach took courage and steely nerves, and most drivers fortified both with ample applications of whiskey.

Most famous of the lot was hard-driving, hard-drinking Hank Monk, whose regular run was the Johnson Pass Road over the Sierra

Monk's trademarks were a battered Stetson, an old corduroy shirt, trousers stained with tobacco juice, and an insatiable thirst. His admirers claimed he could turn a six-horse team in the middle of the road at full gallop, with every line loose. But another observer said, "He drank so much hard spirits that he often forgot what he was doing when it came to the incidental tasks connected with staging, and fed whiskey to his horses and watered himself on numerous occasions.

One night, careening along a rutted road toward Friday's Station, he caught sight of a would-be bandit sneaking out of the brush up ahead. Monk slowed the team to a walk, poured the last of his whiskey over his head, and slumped down in a simulated stupor. When the highwayman saw his condition, he contemptuously ignored the drunken driver and turned to robbing passengers. Monk stealthily grabbed a length of iron pipe and laid the robber out cold. Then he bellowed at his astonished passengers, "All right, you and the bullion is safe, but that bastard cost me my last drink!"

"Pony Bob" Haslam

The Dashing Pony Rider

The Pony Express, most romantic and unique mail service ever devised, captured the imagination of the American public as few events in history have. It is such a colorful part of the lore of the West that few realize it lasted only 18 months, then was replaced by the railroad and the telegraph.

It was organized in 1860 by William Russell and two reluctant backers, to provide weekly mail delivery between St. Joseph, Missouri and Sacramento, California and points between. Because the horses galloped all the way and had to be changed every 12 to 15 miles, a series of 119 relay stations were built.

Riders were unbelievably courageous, crossing mountains and desert, always in danger of marauding Indians. To recruit riders for this dangerous assignment, Russell placed advertisements in newspapers along the frontier: "Wanted...Young, skinny, wiry fellows not over 18. Must be expert riders willing to risk death daily. Orphans preferred." For this, they received $100 a month.

From the numerous applicants he selected 80, one of whom was a 15-year-old fatherless boy named William Cody, who a few years later would be known as Buffalo Bill.

Before a rider was signed up, he had to take a solemn oath not to drink, swear, treat his mounts with cruelty, or fight with hostile Indians. He was then presented with a Bible "to defend himself against moral contamination" and a pair of Colt revolvers.

An average ride for each man was supposed to be 35 miles. But riders sometimes faced stretches of 300 miles, particularly if the next rider was found dead at the station.

"Pony Bob" Haslam

Tales by riders like "Pony Bob" Haslam have become part of the legend of the western frontier. His route was between Lake Tahoe and a place called Buckland, 75 miles to the east. This route was right in the middle of Paiute Indian territory. In his memoirs, Pony Bob recounts one of his most terrifying rides:

"About eight months after the Pony Express was established, the Paiute War commenced in Nevada. Indians could be seen on every mountain peak, and all available men and horses were pressed into service to repel the impending assault.

"When I reached Reed's Station on the Carson River I found no change of horses. I fed the animal I rode and started for the next station. Bucklands was to have been the termination of my journey, but to my astonishment the other rider refused to go on. Within ten minutes I started again. It was a lonely and dangerous ride of 35 miles to the sink of the Carson. I pushed on another 30 miles without a drop of water. At Cold Springs I found to my horror the station had been attacked by Indians."

Pony Bob finished his ride to Smiths Creek, where he was relieved by another rider, then started the return trip to Carson Sink. "It was growing dark and my road lay through sagebrush high enough to hide a horse. I kept a bright outlook and watched my pony's ears, which is a signal for danger in Indian country."

When he arrived at Carson Sink, he found the station men "badly frightened, for they had seen some 50 warriors in warpaint." But Bob took an hour's rest, then assumed his regular run back to the Sierra Nevada mountains.

Another rider named Jim Moore arrived at his station to find the next rider had been killed. He rode for 14 hours and 45 minutes over a distance of 280 miles, an extraordinary feat.

Perhaps the closest call, though, came to two riders named Holt and Wilson, who were at a relay station when about 80 Indians attacked it. When the riders' ammunition ran out the Indians broke down the door and demanded that the two men take all the flour in the station and bake bread. After they had baked most of the day, the Indians tied them to a stake and piled sagebrush at their feet. Fortunately another rider was due in from the West. When he saw what was happening, he quickly rode a few miles back to where he had passed a column of 60 U.S. cavalry troops. Just as Holt and Wilson were about to become more baked than their bread, the cavalry charged over the hill, bugles playing and banners flying, and rescued them.

In all, it took 75 ponies to make the journey from point to point. The well-rested, grain-fed mounts of the Pony Express could usually outrun the grass-fed mounts of the Indians. The service owned 500.

The letters, wrapped in oiled silk to protect them from water, were carried in a leather mochila, a saddlebag that was hung over the saddle and transferred from pony to pony. The

bag had four pockets, three of which were locked at departure points and could be opened only at five points along the route for the removal or addition of letters. The fourth pocket was used for local mail, and could be opened by any station-keeper.

On the first run of the Pony Express, only 25 letters were delivered, at a charge of five dollars per half-ounce. But as news spread of the service's speed and reliability, the numbers began to grow. Correspondents learned to use tissue paper for their messages, and newspapers printed special editions on thin paper for transmission "by pony."

About the time the Pony Express began attracting sizable amounts of mail, some government officials were spending as much as $135 a letter. Congress was pressed to cut expenses, so funds were appropriated to complete the rail line from Omaha to California.

By Pony

PONY EXPRESS
25 CTS ½ OZ.
ENCLOSED IN OUR FRANK
WELLS FARGO & CO.

25¢ a half-ounce

When railroads began stringing wires along their right-of-ways to carry messages sent by Samuel Morse's amazing new invention, the days of the Pony Express were over.

The dashing Pony Express rider gallops past the line that will soon replace him.

"Snowshoe" Thompson
The Legendary Mailman

Most remarkable and fearless of mountaineers in the Sierra Nevada mountains of 1859, was the Norwegian, John "Snowshoe" Thompson, who brought skiing to America.

For twenty years, when the Comstock silver mine was at its peak, Thompson undertook delivery of mail from Sacramento, California to Virginia City, Nevada, on promise of a mail delivery contract. It was perhaps the worst possible mail route in the history of the West.

Thompson was a 30-year-old farmer in Sacramento when he read that mail delivery over the Sierra had been suspended for the winter, due to snow levels that were 60 feet deep. That didn't seem too bad to this hardy Norwegian. Where he had grown up, snow never stopped anyone.

So from the memory of his boyhood, he fashioned a pair of "Norwegian snowshoes." Unlike the bear-paw type of Canadian snowshoes familiar to Westerners, these were 10-foot runners made of oak. Holding a long balance pole in front of him, like a tight-rope walker, he flew down mountain slopes with the ease of an eagle soaring. On promise of a mail delivery contract, he started delivering letters across the Sierra mountains to miners in Nevada. For 50 cents a pound, he delivered clothing and mining supplies.

He carried no blankets. He wore no overcoat. At nightfall, he fashioned pine boughs into a lean-to, huddled by a fire in a hollow tree log, or danced on a flat rock to keep from freezing.

While on the move he would dip into a small packet of beef jerky and hardtack. Usually it took him three days for his 90-mile trip up the hill, and two days to return downhill. His compass was the stars.

For nearly twenty years he regularly made an incredible two to four round trips a month alone, in defiance of blizzard, avalanche, and wild animals. He always set out on the day appointed, without regard for weather, often carrying up to 100 pounds.

"I have found a great many lost men," Thompson once said, "and have rescued some when they were at death's door."

One such desperate man was James Sisson. Thompson discovered him, quite by accident, in a deserted cabin in the Lake Valley region of Lake Tahoe, just before Christmas in 1866. Sisson had been there twelve days; his feet were frozen in his boots, purple almost to the knees. He was unable to move, and was considering amputating his own legs with an axe he found in the cabin. Thompson lighted a fire and made Sisson as comfortable as possible, then got on his skis and traveled all night to get to the nearest town for help. There he raised a party of eight men, fashioned skis for them plus a sled for Sisson. They reached the cabin by that evening.

It took them two days to travel the 10 miles back to the village of Genoa, due to a terrific storm. There, doctors said they'd have to amputate, but they had no chloroform. So the rawboned Norwegian started back over the Sierra on his 25-lb. skis. The round trip to Sacramento took five days, when he was back in Genoa with the chloroform.

There were times, during the Civil War, when Thompson was the only link between California and the Union. In addition to mail delivery, he rescued sick and injured, carried food to snowbound families, delivered medicines and lamp chimneys, mining supplies and a crystal ball for a seeress, and even a font of newspaper type for Nevada's first newspaper, the "Territorial Enterprise."

He was never paid by the U.S. government for his years of mail delivery service. He had been promised a contract and an appointment, but they were never forthcoming. He died at the age of 49, still trying to collect.

He is buried in Genoa, Nevada, a small Sierra Nevada village. At the base of his tombstone is a plaque, placed there by the Norwegian ski team of the 1960 Olympics at Squaw Valley, commemorating "our fellow skier from Telemark."

William Cody
Fabled Buffalo Bill

"When your joints are cold and stiff, and an old pony is doing his double best to unload you, a cowboy don't feel none too happy," lamented the buckaroo.

———————

There was little that was romantic about a cowboy's life. It took "Buffalo Bill" Cody to create a heroic image for him. When Cody featured the exploits of cowboys and Indians in his Wild West show, his portrayal of the cowboy set the pattern for a hundred novels and motion pictures yet to come.

Will Cody was born in Iowa. He had little schooling, was subjected spasmodically to some book learning, but was released from all that when his father "took gold fever" and headed for California. The family never got there. At Kansas City the father died, leaving 11-year-old Will with his mother, five sisters and a baby brother to support.

He had a hard time finding work, but finally got a job cleaning out stables. Almost immediately he showed a rapport with horses, a talent that would mold his life.

THE HORSELESS HEAD MAN: It appears some varmint stole his horse.

A succession of jobs followed, all involving horses. At fifteen he was hired by the Pony Express. The wages were good, and he was valuable to them, being a good rider and experienced on the trail.

His route was 76 miles long, with the North Platte River to ford along the way. One day he was ambushed by Indians but thought he had managed to outrun them to the next relay station. When he got there he discovered the Indians had already been there, killing the attendant and taking the ponies.

His next job was with the Kansas Pacific Railroad, supplying buffalo meat to feed construction crews. During the next eighteen months he killed more than 4,000 head, thus acquiring his nickname of "Buffalo Bill." He also acquired, along with other buffalo hunters, the fierce hostility of Indians, whose food supply was being decimated.

About this time a hack writer named Ned Buntline came west in search of material on which to base some Wild West tales. In Cody he found the prototype he sought for his highly colored "true" stories to be published in "dime novels" — forerunner of the paperback.

The books were an immediate success, sweeping "Buffalo Bill" along in a glowing aura of glory.

Buntline dressed his hero in fancy, long-fringed buckskins, braided and beaded boots, and a wide sombrero. For the rest of his life, Will Cody lived his character. He acted in stage melodramas about the West in winter, worked as a scout or hunting guide in summer.

In 1883 he created Buffalo Bill's Wild West Show and became its star attraction. Over six feet tall and arrow-straight, he made a commanding presence on stage as the company toured form one fairground to another across the country. Eventually the show reached every U.S. capital and some in Europe.

At each stop, the entire outfit was unloaded — cowboys, Indians, buffalo, elk, mountain sheep, wild horses, stagecoach and all. From the first, Cody insisted on absolute realism. Actors were genuine frontiersmen, Indians were recruited personally by Cody from the reservations.

These talent searches were great occasions in the lives of the Indians. As Death Valley Scotty told it, "The ceremony became an annual spring affair, with Cody selecting the lucky individuals. The Indians, five or six hundred of them, would come to the town where auditions were to be held, dressed in their finest buckskins, feathers and beads. They were quite a sight in their gaudy finery. Only a small number could be used, and those not chosen felt bad. The government required bonds be posted that the Indians would be well fed while away, and would be returned to the reservation in good health and a new suit of clothes.

"They left the reservation in paint and feathers, and returned a year later in Prince Albert coats, Stetsons, patent leather shoes, and long, well-groomed glossy hair."

In the presentation of an Indian attack on the Deadwood stagecoach and the rescue by himself and his men, Cody insisted on complete authenticity. The only thing *not* permitted was killing and scalping. The four mules that drew the coach were wild and hard to handle, barely broken to the harness. So Cody hired as the driver one of the oldest and best-known drivers on western stage routes.

He even recruited Sitting Bull, who welcomed the release from the tedium and confinement of reservation life. He attracted tremendous crowds, earning for Buffalo Bill many times over the fifty dollars per week the showman paid him. Boos and catcalls sometimes sounded for the "Killer of Custer," but after each show these same people pressed coins upon him for copies of his signed photograph. (A friendly Canadian trader had taught him how to write his name in English.)

In October when the tour ended, newsmen asked the Chief what he thought of the cities he'd seen. "The tipi is better," he told them. "I am sick of the houses and the noises and the multitude of men."

The show went on for thirty years, through good times and bad. During this long period Cody made a lot of money and spent a lot of money, mainly on luxurious living. He drank heavily (his favorite drink was a shot of rye and a twist of lemon in a glass of cider), sometimes to the detriment of his performance. Though he had a reputation for being generous, he wasn't a good businessman, and let a couple of fortunes slip through his fingers.

———

When he died in Denver during World War I at the age of 71, he was broke and alone. At his own request, he was buried atop Lookout Mountain, and became in death one of Colorado's biggest tourist draws.

He would have liked that.

All this action actually went on during a performance.